Keys for Kingdom Power
Sharon Reynolds

© 2024 by Sharon Reynolds

Published by Holy Spirit Happenings

All rights reserved. No part of this book may be reproduced by any mechanical, photographic, or electronic process or in the form of a phonographic recording; nor may it be stored in a retrieval system, transmitted, or otherwise be copied for public or private use – other than "fair use" as brief quotations embodied in articles and reviews – without prior written permission of the publisher.

This publication is intended to provide helpful and informative material on the subjects addressed. The author's intent is only to offer information of a general nature to help you on your journey for emotional and spiritual well-being. Readers should consult their health professionals before adopting any of the suggestions in this book, either directly or indirectly. If you use any of the information in this book for yourself, the author and the publisher expressly disclaim any adverse effects from applying the published information.

Unless otherwise noted, Scripture quotations are taken from THE HOLY BIBLE, ENGLISH STANDARD VERSION (ESV): Scriptures taken from THE HOLY BIBLE, ENGLISH STANDARD VERSION ® Copyright© 2001 by Crossway, a publishing ministry of Good News Publishers. Used by permission. Scriptures marked KJV are taken from the KING JAMES VERSION (KJV): KING JAMES VERSION, public domain. Scriptures marked NKJV are taken from the NEW KING JAMES VERSION (NKJV): Scripture taken from the NEW KING JAMES VERSION®. Copyright© 1982 by Thomas Nelson, Inc. Used by permission. All rights reserved.

Paperback ISBN: 978-1-0670045-0-7; Ebook ISBN: 978-1-0670045-1-4

Cover design by Barbi Larkins | Be Design

I dedicate this book to the loving memory of my son, Shaun Connor Reynolds, who has always inspired me to grow in faith.

From death to life, He is Risen!

Whatever you have been through. Whatever you are currently facing. There is an answer. For all the hurt and loss. For all the hopes deferred and dreams delayed. Even for those most devastating and tragic moments that seemed best dealt with by burying them forever. But I promise you, there is an answer to all of it. His name is Jesus. He has healing for you. He has restoration for you. He even has a way of redeeming the time and turning it all to the good. I know that can be hard to believe amidst all the tears, disappointment, anger, questions, and numbness. But it is true. And it's why I am so grateful for Sharon Reynolds and the book *Keys for Kingdom Power*.

In these pages, Sharon guides you to that truth, and even more, she guides you to Him who is The Truth. The Truth of Healing. The Truth of hope, joy, peace, and the fullness of life restored. The Truth that there is something on the other side of the hurt. Healing, yes. But even more than that. Life restored. Life fulfilled. Glorious life!

Start into Keys for Kingdom Power right now, and let the healing, revival, and renewal begin as Sharon leads you into revelation and encounter with The One who can truly turn it all to the good!

Robert Hotchkin

Founder, Robert Hotchkin Ministries / Men on the Frontlines/ Host, Supernatural Mentoring Series, roberthotchkin.com

Foreword

Inside my mailbox sat a very large cheque. I had been notified by the sender that it had been delivered and was awaiting pick up. I was excited to receive it but had a big problem – I couldn't find the key to open my mailbox. I looked high and low for it, but sadly, it was nowhere to be found.

Even though the mailbox was my personal mailbox with my name assigned to it, I could not open it as I did not have the key. I could not access the contents even though they belonged to me. No key – no access. The cheque had the potential to help many people and advance Kingdom mandates, but I could not access any of the potential because I did not have the key.

We contacted the postal company, which, after verification, came and changed the lock and made new keys for me. I finally could access the cheque and hold its potential in my hands.

Many believers have great blessings waiting for pick up. However, they do not hold the key(s) required to open the door to the Kingdom power they desperately need. As a result, they live in frustration and want.

Two thousand years ago, Jesus died on the cross and established a holy covenant between God and man that was sealed in His own blood. This binding agreement is an eternal, unbreakable covenant of love offering unsearchable Kingdom riches, power, blessings, and promises in the Lord for everyone who believes in Christ.

Jesus is the Master Key. He can and will open every door of revelation, desire, opportunity, and Kingdom insight and essence to all who follow Him. As I was praying into writing this foreword, the Holy Spirit gave me a visionary image of a key ring, and on the ring, there was one large, gold Master Key. He drew me close to behold the key ring and the Master Key. As I gazed at them, suddenly, from inside the large master key came numerous smaller keys. All of them were attached to the key ring but had come forth from the Master Key.

The Holy Spirit then guided me through the spiritual encounter and unfolded a vision of a corridor filled with many doors. Each door represented a Kingdom realm that could be accessed and opened only by keys on the ring. In the encounter, I saw the key ring in my hand. I possessed every key needed to open every door into the realms of the Kingdom. All I had to do was use them, and doors of encounter would open.

Sharon Reynold's book, Keys for Kingdom Power, will place this divine key ring in your hand. She brilliantly defines various keys and gives practical guidance on using them to open doors to Kingdom realities and encounters.

I love Sharon's passion for believers to access all the Lord has for them. She herself has walked through many challenging seasons in her life and has discovered keys that brought perspective, freedom, and power. She now presents those keys to you. The keys she reveals in this book will open realms of Kingdom encounter and empowerment for you. Your journey into a new season of glorious discovery begins.

Patricia King

Author, Minister, Media Host

www.patriciaking.com

Preface

How do I tell the story, the revelation I'm ready to share? Where do I even begin?

Sitting at my writing table, surrounded by blaring music, I'm delving deep to find the proper beginning for a tale nearly too unbelievable to speak of. I look at the pile of change sitting on my desk, and I'm reminded that these are the stories I must tell. People are waiting in the balance for God to set them free, and He's entrusted the scribal pen to me.

I'm reflecting on how much my life changed in a literal moment. That change on my desk was the last prophecy I gave before my son's tragic death, mere months before I wrote this book, the third in my series of Kingdom Revelations.

One moment, I was on a Zoom call, and the next, the sounds of first responders' sirens interrupted me. As usual, I took a moment to pray for the sounds I heard during the meeting. Thirty minutes later, I opened the front door to the police, informing me about an incident.

The incident they were referring to was the death of my eighteen-year-old son, Shaun. A train had hit him on his way to work, and the sounds I heard and responded to in prayer were in response to his life ending. Despite the tragedy and hardship, God was by my side, encouraging me to tell the stories He entrusted me with, even through my grieving hours. Stories of mothers and sons, of love and overcoming. Of the miraculous and His resurrection power.

Experiencing God's healing made me realise there are mothers in the Bible with stories that hold the keys to many people's liberation. I have a mandate to help free the captives, so I brought this book to life. It's dedicated to seeing hearts come alive.

> *"The Spirit of the Lord God is upon Me, Because the Lord has anointed Me To preach good tidings to the poor; He has sent Me to heal the brokenhearted, To proclaim liberty to the captives, And the opening of the prison to those who are bound;" (Isaiah 61)*

This book is filled with the hope and healing power that Jesus's name brings to every situation. With every word you consume, I pray hope ignites within you, unveiling the immense love of a Father who cherishes you.

Living in heavenly places, we understand our power and authority as sons and daughters. The keys to the Kingdom I'm passing along will help you access the fullness of being His child and bringing heaven to earth.

Once, I dreamt of a mansion. I saw myself as a child running in corridors. Many rooms hosted magnificent experiences. Glory overwhelmed me as I explored, amazed by everything. Angels surrounded me, radiating joy, peace, and love from every part of their being. Then, I stopped to ponder. How did I get access to all the rooms in the mansion? I inquired of the Lord, and He replied that there was no need for keys to enter my Father's house. As I am His child, I have free rein in all areas of Him. Now, let's bring heaven to earth!

This, my friend, is your invitation to sit with God and reflect on what He has to say to you through me.

Acknowledgements

My first acknowledgment is always to thank God in all I do. He is worthy of the praise and honour and gets all the Glory for everything I put my hands to.

To Craig Reynolds, my husband, biggest supporter, and greatest fan, thank you for your commitment to picking up your cross and loving me daily.

To my children, Jessica, Catherine, Lydia, Daniel, Shaun, and Amy, thank you for being such cool kids!

To all those who have supported me in this journey and my ministry colleagues, I thank you for your unwavering love and earnest prayers.

Thank you to Patricia King, Robert Hotchkin, and Wendy Peter for their incredible mentoring and loving support.

Special thanks also to my local pastors, Steven and Patience Pona, and to all those in the worldwide church family of God who have walked through Shaun's death and resurrection with me and my family. Your love has carried us well. We are forever grateful for you all.

Introduction

My intention was never to write books solely for Christians. The goal was to reveal the transformative power of God's love and inspire and heal the world through my adventures and encounters with Jesus. But while writing, I realised Christians needed these messages as much, if not more, than those without faith in Christ. I discovered that the Church desperately needs hope and healing.

Holy Spirit has revealed the keys to releasing people from their afflictions and troubles. Be assured, beloved, that I have walked out and worked out every single key in this book myself before it arrived in your hands. You now hold the keys to advancing your destiny because of what God has done.

As always, I remain thankful that God trusts me as His voice and that I hold His pen in my hand. The glory is all His.

My family is my strength. They celebrate every victory with me and walk alongside me, finding joy in being who I am! I pray the same blessings for you as you grow in your walk with God.

I'm always grateful for each person I meet and encounter with God's love. It's an honour to be part of His great family and serve as His scribe. I earnestly pray that you will find a way through whatever situation you face today and discover everlasting joy!

I wrote this book for every broken woman who's encountered any form of trauma and loss in her life. God kept crying out to me to go after the desperate ones. Send me, O Lord! As you read, you'll encounter keys that will set you free. Pray with faith, believe God's word, and watch as truth manifests in your life.

Then consider that your freedom comes at a great price. You now hold the power to see others freed from desperate circumstances and afflictions of the heart and mind, with many ways to get there. Seek God with how you are to respond and activate the resurrection power you have encountered in these pages, in Jesus' name.

Contents

1. Blind Faith — 1
2. Obedience = Blessings — 11
3. Resurrection Power — 15
4. Identity in Christ — 23
5. A Royal Inheritance — 37
6. New Miracles — 47
7. The Father's Table — 55
8. Greater Authority — 65
9. Alive in Christ — 75

Afterword — 87

About the Author — 89

Other Books by Sharon Reynolds — 91

10. Glory Realms — 93

1
Blind Faith

Hear me, O LORD, hear me, that this people may know that You are the LORD God, and that You have turned their hearts back to You again. 1 KINGS 18:37

Following a message I had just preached, where I issued a challenge to stand against fear, God called me up into the mountains to be with Him. Back in my room, I followed His first instructions to eat, drink, and rest. I drifted off and dreamt of the Prophet Elisha's encounter with a widow woman in 2 Kings 4. In the Bible story and my dream, God used this woman to provide food and rest for the prophet. As I had just been obedient to the Lord by preaching His message, He now called me as His prophet away to rest.

As I made my way to my accommodation in the mountains, a divine encounter awaited me when I stopped to use the public toilets. I happened upon a woman I'd not seen in at least a year since her marriage ended, and here she was, in the middle of nowhere! During our conversation, she shared that despite the financial and emotional challenges that she, her children, and her ex-husband endured, it had all prompted her to reconnect with her faith.

Knowing this family, this was truly remarkable! I embraced her tightly and conveyed my sorrow for the situation and my enthusiasm for her and her family's future now that God was involved. We prayed together for both her ex-husband and herself, then parted ways.

***

Upon arriving at the mountain retreat, I flipped through scripture to find 2 Kings 4, eager to read more about the Prophet Elisha and the desperate widow woman he encountered. This poor woman was facing potential bondage if she didn't pay a large debt that was owed.

Reading their story, I vividly imagined a prophet peacefully resting in a small hut. The widow woman appeared before him in a dire situation. Her husband had died, leaving her alone with two sons. If the woman did not pay the husband's debt in full straight away, a creditor planned to take her sons as payment. The boys would become slaves for him to do with however he wanted.

A jar of oil was all she had in the world. How could she possibly pay off her debt with one jar of oil? Elisha instructed her to gather empty vessels from anywhere, even borrowing if necessary. She was to collect as many as possible. He sent her out, and she showed faith through action by obediently completing the task. Elisha hadn't explained the plan for the empty vessels yet, so she was operating in blind faith, trusting his instructions, knowing somehow it was the right thing to do.

Blind faith is equal to obedience.

Has there been a time when God presented you with an opportunity, and you blindly followed, or did you doubt? Was an increase of faith needed or obedience? That is a question for you and you alone to answer, but take a moment to consider it before you read on.

***

You see, the prophet knew all she had was a single jar of oil—Scripture says, "a small flask." Yet Elisha ordered her to borrow vessels from all her neighbours—not just a few, but all. What would these vessels be used for? This demonstrates that he was setting her up for success.

What we can take from this is that when God gives you a command, you mustn't focus on what you don't have. You need to make room for the unseen, what you *will* have. The widow woman had but one jar for capturing oil, but little did she know she was making room for more.

Elisha then gave the woman and her two sons instructions. "Shut the door" (2 Kings 4:4)! In the next verse, she poured out the vessels, and what happened next was nothing short of a miracle. You're saying a woman, a widow woman at that, was performing a miracle? Yes! She filled every vessel she had with oil, one after another.

How could she be filling the empty containers with oil, you might be asking? Where was the oil coming from? Great question! The door to the house was completely shut, and no one else was near her, meaning she was actually producing the oil from within her hands, where she held the one small flask. Are you saying it was flowing from the flask in her hands? Yes! She continued to pour oil until she filled every vessel she had collected. Then the oil ceased to flow (4:6).

When she completed her mission, she returned to Elisha and told him what had happened. He instructed her to leave and sell the abundance of oil to pay off her debt. Then, with the increase left over, she could live happily with her sons. The sales of the oil were more than enough to set them free. Her sons didn't have to become slaves; they had enough money to continue living well. Their destiny was to live freely and abundantly, not destitute or enslaved. Hallelujah!

***

This amazing and miraculous story has many layers of revelation. You see, the widow woman found herself in a desperate situation. Her husband died owing money, and his outstanding debt fell on the family he left behind. Like many mothers in desperate times, the woman considered her options for preventing a horrendous outcome. She had no money. No one to help her. Nothing left but a desperate cry. So, she went to the prophet for help with but one small jar of oil.

All too often around the world, I have seen desperate women do desperate things to survive and provide for their children. I have been one of those desperate women in days gone by. I understand the hardship that many encounter. Thankfully, Christ has redeemed my past and restored my dignity and worth. And if you're reading this right now and you're one of these women, I want to assure you that He can do the same for you. No one is beyond His repair.

The other lesson here is that the Prophet Elisha saw the solution before it manifested. Seer Prophets, in particular, don't see the same way others do with their visual eyes. They tend to see ahead. In other words, they're not looking at the problem before them because they already have the solution. They're often ahead and around the corner before others have even taken the first step. So, although the Hebrew text says it was "but a flask of oil," a minuscule amount, Elisha saw what it would become, which was an answer and a blessing.

***

Can you imagine what it must have been like for the widow woman to stand there pouring endless oil from a small flask in her hand? Container after container, she poured as her sons moved the full ones aside, ushering in the next vessel. I don't know about you and your family, but I can tell you my kids and I would have been screaming and rejoicing in wonder and amazement!

Then, all of a sudden, the oil stopped flowing. In the Hebrew text, it says the oil "stood up." That's not a physical, literal meaning, but a metaphorical term used in economic markets, meaning the oil price rose simultaneously as she received her miracle. So, she received a double blessing. Not only had miraculous oil solved her problem, but its value increased. As it increased, the widow's obedience was rewarded at a higher price. That's abundant living right there!

What the enemy could have accomplished in trying to steal, kill, and destroy, he did not! He could have stolen her sons to pay the debt. He could have held her in bondage and killed her hope, and as a woman alone in that society, she may have even died. Or he could have destroyed her family and future prophets, along with her family's future. He could've taken her reputation through forced acts, just like countless other women all over the world today endure. However, none of that had to happen. Instead, the widow was blessed with the best possible outcome because of her faith, trust, and obedience.

***

Just as I went up the mountain with little, God gave me much in return. In my time with the Lord, He showed me the layers of this woman's miraculous story and reminded me of a debt my father had, which was keeping my own family in bondage. When my father passed away years earlier, there was an outstanding debt my mother had refused to pay out of her desperation for financial sustainability. God revealed right then and there that the family debt had to be wiped clean for my freedom and my children's inherited freedom. If we did not reconcile it, we would continue to live in financial and spiritual bondage.

I was still at the mountain retreat when I called my mother and told her she should settle the debt immediately. Although she hesitated, she miraculously decided to release the funds and pay the debt in full. She described afterward that she sensed being set free when she did this, with the heavy burden no longer falling upon her. At that moment, the burden was also lifted from both myself and my household. Freedom!

Following God's instructions, I called my mother that night, ensuring future generations would be saved from a destructive debt. I believe God wants us to learn from my experience in the mountains. It started with running into a woman from my past who turned to God in desperation because of her failed marriage. It ended with a desperate woman paying her debt in full and, in turn, setting a generation free from bondage caused by an unpaid debt. The revelation of God in His Word set all this in motion. God always weaves the truth of His Word into my life, just as I weave these stories together while walking out my faith and obedience, like the story of Elisha and the widow woman.

Kingdom Keys

1. Faith—Trust God's Word regardless of the desperation of your circumstances.

2. Obedience—Trust His instructions to you. Walk everything out with the Holy Spirit.

3. Make room for Miracles—Activate faith in the unseen by going forth! God does the impossible with us to show His manifest presence.

4. Expect—Get in a position to receive and be ready for the increase!

The next day, in my mountain retreat, I awoke and made a fresh pot of coffee. As I did, I turned to see a small flask hanging on the wall next to me! Yes, that's right. To my amazement, it was an actual flask, like the widow woman had! It was as if God was reaching beyond the veil, between the realms of heaven and earth, speaking to me loud and clear.

I observed how someone had etched a small fantail into the outside of the flask. I noted God always speaks to me about how much He provides for the birds of the air. And how they don't go hungry or without shelter. If so, how much more does He care for us than them? How much more will He provide for us?

I called a close friend to share this exciting moment and explained what God revealed in the story the night before. She was right about what she said about the flask on the wall. "I bet there's oil in it." It smelled of fragrant oil, but I couldn't open the lid. However, this was symbolic of what the Lord had shown me. That the time for multiplication miracles was upon me now. I had NZD 10,000 in my business account. I knew that if I poured this small flask of oil (representing money) into empty vessels, I would see an increase.

***

Now that I was free from the bondage of my inherited debt, I took the little bit of money in my account and metaphorically poured it out to produce my second book, *The Kingdom Within*. That "oil" also flowed enough to support an African woman in her business endeavours and missionary work for the next four years. It not only became possible for me to help her financially, but the funds kept multiplying and spreading further, transforming the lives of her entire village, even through COVID-19. *The Kingdom Within* sold hundreds of copies worldwide, allowing even more women to gain freedom. The Lord poured and poured.

The African women represented my empty vessels, and my blessing became our mutual wealth. I began dreaming about micro-businesses and women sewing bags. The visions inspired me to design a special bag with a padded handle to help ease these women's uncomfortable burdens. I shared with my

African friend all my ideas of seeing small enterprises set up throughout Kenya. The message God gave me needed to be shared with others: These businesses would free the captives, releasing people from their spiritual and physical debt and increasing their resources.

***

Another dream I had one night also resulted in God setting an employee free from *their* debt. Despite cutting ties with a company we had been partnering with because of internal issues that no longer aligned with our business values, this staff member joined one of my contract holders without informing me. However, this staff member had hidden the fact that they had accepted an external offer and carried on working for that company on an ad hoc basis. The agreements with this person and the contract holders included a restraint of trade clause. This clause prohibited them from working with my staff for at least six months after they left my company.

It was a standard clause, bringing me annoyance and a lack of trust in the person. I had the legal right to address them and the company, and even though they asked me to work with them again, I declined. This type of behaviour was not what I wanted in my company, nor did I want to align God's finances with it. As I prayed on how to go about handling the situation, the Lord gave me a word of knowledge of sexual sin in the staff member's marriage.

God exposed this person's shame, as they feared my knowledge of the truth. As I sat and had the hard discussion, the truth won, and repentance came forth. God showed me step-by-step that it was in my hands to forgive the debt and the betrayal. As I released what was owed to me, I became a blessing to that person, setting them free from any bondage I could have held them to. Just like the desperate woman who went to the prophet, God revealed that we, too, can forgive debts owed to us and others. "And be kind to one another, tenderhearted, forgiving one another, just as God in Christ forgave you" (Ephesians 4:23).

We, as children of God, possess greater power than Elisha. Yes, he gave the woman a miracle that accompanied her faith, providing a way out of enslavement. But we have Jesus Christ, who paid every debt for us. We are now to forgive our trespassers, releasing them from bondage, as Christ has forgiven us and set us free. We must forgive as we have been forgiven. "And forgive us our debts, As we forgive our debtors" (Matthew 6:12).

Pray this prayer with me now:

Father, I come to you in the name of Jesus and ask that you forgive all debts owed by me and to me by the miracle-working power that you have given to those who believe. As I proclaim this day that I believe in you and your son Jesus Christ, I partake of the blessing of the power to forgive any debt and to have all my debts forgiven. Holy Spirit, release those who have been held in captivity from the bondage of debt now, including myself, in Jesus' Name. Amen.

2
Obedience = Blessings

If you are willing and obedient, you will eat the good things of the land. ISAIAH 1:19

Let's move on to the next desperate woman and situation: Elijah and the widow woman. We know from reading scripture that Elijah heard from God directly in every moment of life. Because the Lord ordered each step he took, Elijah truly lived in complete faith. The Hebrew text says, "This word of Adonai came to him." God can speak to us by giving commands, sending angels to do His will, and through direct messages.

In 1 Kings 17:12, during a drought in Sidon, God sent Elijah from his resting place by a brook, where he was fed by ravens day and night, to dwell (stay awhile, habituate, live) in a famine-stricken land with no food. He obeyed. God then told Elijah He would send him a widow woman to provide for him, a widow who did not worship or believe in the God of Israel, Yahweh.

When Elijah arrived at the city gates, he saw a woman and asked her to bring him water and bread. She explained her dire situation to him. That she only had enough food for one last meal for herself and her son, and then death was imminent. That's all she could see for her future, and she resigned herself to the outcome. All other options had run out.

Elijah told the widow to continue preparing the meal and gathering sticks for a fire but to set aside a small loaf of bread for him. Imagine the fear of this woman, alone with a man, not of her culture or town. He was a total stranger, telling her she must feed him while preparing for her death and the death of her son. I'm sure she had to feel quite vulnerable and scared, with no one to help or protect her should things begin to go the wrong way in an instant.

***

How many times have we seen women being attacked, subdued, or taken from their towns and homes through the simple act of stopping to answer a question from a stranger walking by or innocently giving directions to someone on the side of a road who looks lost? For a woman outside the city gates, this was a tremendous risk!

The woman told Elijah she only had a little oil in a jar, enough to cook just once (1 Kings 17:12). Let's stop and pause there momentarily. Have you noticed that we're about to see the same principle demonstrated for multiplication with this oil? Both widows had very little. However, unlike the previous widow woman, who was married to a prophet's servant and educated in his prophetic school, this widow did not have a relationship with God.

Elijah then gave her a word from the Lord, telling her not to fear. "Go home and do as you have said. But first, make a small loaf of bread for me from what you have and bring it to me, and then make something for yourself and your son. For this is what the Lord, the God of Israel, says: 'The jar of flour will not be used up and the jug of oil will not run dry until the day the Lord sends rain on the land'" (1 Kings 17:13-14 NIV).

After hearing from God, whom she did not previously believe in, the widow followed the instructions given to her in blind faith and obedience. Because of her obedience, she maintained continual provision until rain broke the three-year drought. Amid a famine, the widow, her son, and their community ate abundantly and supernaturally for many years. Not one perished. This shows us that God manifests His unlimited goodness through those who believe *and* those who do not.

The Prophet Elijah's obedience ensured his well-being and allowed him to bless a woman in desperate need. Through him, the next generation was saved and also blessed. God can use anything and anyone to bring about a turnaround. Imagine the impact on their community! We see that when you sacrifice to God in obedience, He honours and multiplies it. By sacrificing part of her meal for Elijah, the widow woman experienced incredible supernatural multiplication. Resurrection power brings life from death.

Kingdom Keys

1. Elijah was obedient. He took action. Obedience brings blessings.

2. God provided ahead of time for Elijah, as He does for all His people. He doesn't send you forth without provision for the journey and assignment.

3. God can bless even those who do not believe. He is not limited.

4. As God's people, we are to be a blessing to those around us.

Pause and consider this story, seeking guidance from God on how to use the oil in your possession. How can you be a blessing to others? Can you aid in bringing others from death to life, liberating those in captivity? Ask Him to show you.

Just like our first two widows, God welcomes both believers and unbelievers. He pours out miracles on all, with the purpose of faith arising and belief coming forth. As I sat up the mountain with the Lord, I realised He was showing me that grace is favour. Grace is favour when you don't deserve it, regardless of who you are, what you've done, or even what you believe. God will deliver you, no matter what. That is God's favour!

As you continue to read this book, you may receive a challenge from God to move from your current place and take action. Your mission is to help free those affected by life's misfortunes and believe in the miraculous transformation of entire communities, both spiritually and physically. I decree and declare the resurrection power of wealth and abundance to the widows and fatherless among the generations.

I encourage you to steward what you have well and witness the increase in blessings. God has entrusted you with territory to help every person you've dreamed of helping. Use your testimony and the Blood of the Lamb to overcome. Share these powerful stories with others and witness God's work with your *little oil*.

Decree:

I believe in the miraculous transformation of entire communities, both spiritually and physically, by the power of God.

This is the resurrection power of Heaven manifest in all the earth.

3
Resurrection Power

The Lord is not slack concerning His promise, as some count slackness, but is longsuffering toward us, not willing that any should perish but that all should come to repentance.
2 PETER 3:9

Our next story is about Resurrection Power. The first two chapters showed two mothers in desperate positions. One had given up hope while preparing for death, while the other pursued an answer. We saw how both women's faith arose through miraculous provision, enabling the women and their families to be set free.

Let's now revisit the woman from Sidon whom God sent to Elijah (1 Kings 17-24) and talk about her son, who encountered the prophet and had his life spared during the famine.

Sometime after the flour and oil miracle, the widow's son became seriously sick and died. When Elijah arrived on the scene, she thought the man of God was there to remind her about the sin of her past that she shamefully believed caused her son to die. But that wasn't the case. Elijah stepped in, taking the child upstairs and pleading with God for the boy to live. After all that had happened, how could he now die? In a strange sequence of events, Elijah laid on the boy three times and miraculously brought him back to life.

Elijah prayed, "Adonai, my God, please let this child's soul return to him." Then, he witnessed the child's resurrection! He took the boy back downstairs to his mother, now alive! Elijah handed him over to her, and she exclaimed, "Now I know you are a man of God, and the word of Adonai that you speak is the truth."

Now, personally, I would think years of food from a little oil and flour would have been enough for me to believe. But okay, that wasn't the case with her. What *really* convinced the woman from Sidon was bringing her dead child back to life because that was her heart's desire.

Sometimes the miracle of sustenance is only enough for the soul. What brings people back to God is the resurrection power of love.

***

The woman became a believer after this miracle! Scripture also denotes that this incident proved Elijah's integrity, and his word was forevermore acknowledged as God's word. The woman experienced the benefits of the prophet's company in the first part of her story (1 Kings 17:8-16), which was an ongoing food supply. However, because in her culture, her gods would punish people or become angry to the point of afflicting them, she presumed her sins caused her son's illness and inevitable death. She then experienced the benefits of being in the presence of the glory of God.

The prophet's presence carried divine scrutiny for those around him because anyone near him experienced the glory falling on them. Darkness cannot exist at that level of light. Such has been the case in my life. As the anointing increased, my children kept getting caught lying and stealing. They continuously got sprung! The kids cleaned up their acts, or they couldn't bear to be in my company for long.

It isn't personal when this happens; it's the glory of God that you carry. As the anointing increases, those around you will feel it, and their sin will be exposed, especially when the miraculous moves through you with incomprehensible intensity.

Elijah knew the level of God's anointing he carried, and as a result, the child in this story also became a glory carrier of God's presence. God sent Elijah to bring abundant life to the woman and child. He first performed an incredible miracle of provision, and yet she still didn't follow God. It took some time and a second miracle, but her love for her son eventually led her to believe.

Some become complacent and overlook God's role, yet here we see He was the sole solution. So, what will it take for you to believe? Not everyone who receives God's goodness will follow Him straight away, and sadly, some will just outright reject Him, but we who believe are to remain hopeful.

***

I returned to my Bible, and a young woman I knew closely from Papua New Guinea suddenly contacted me. She was now twenty-five, had made some poor choices, and had travelled off her path of destiny and fellowship with God. This young woman had been a Sunday school teacher just six short years before this moment she reached out. At nineteen, she was full of life and a godly leader in her community. What had gone wrong?

She shared about her relationship problems, which meant a *man problem*. I felt prompted to ask her hard questions and speak the truth to help set her free. I extended an invitation for her to come back to God and reminded her that both of us love her dearly. Agreeing that was true, she thanked me, saying she really needed to hear that. I then prayed with her, and she thanked me again with tears in her eyes. She declared that she was a changed person from that night on and walked back to the right path.

I knew the love of the Father, but she needed a mother's heart. She revealed to me later that she was feeling extremely low and desperate that night and came very close to ending her life. Suddenly, my face appeared on her Facebook screen, and she felt compelled to reach out. She'd lost contact with her community because of her choices, and her mother was a widow who didn't have the strength to provide what her daughter needed.

God loves us so much. She needed someone to talk to, and God brought me to her. Like the woman of Sidon, struggling with life outside the walls and security of her city, this young woman was also walking outside of her belief system. She needed a word from the Lord delivered through a prophetic mouth to help turn her around. People can have great experiences of the miraculous in their lives, but some need a deeper heart encounter.

***

I felt God's presence, but what I didn't know at the time was that it was the love of my daughter, who was facing death through depression, that opened the way for God to really start moving in my life. God is no respecter of circumstances. He always swoops in, regardless of the situation you find yourself in.

Did the woman of Sidon deserve God's unmerited favour? Not particularly, but maybe. Did I? Do you? Who are we to decide? Does it even matter? No, it doesn't. Why not? Because God's love doesn't keep an account of your wrongs. It's that despite your wrongs, He loves you.

The woman of Sidon knew what her sins were and, with deep shame, thought they cost her son's life. How gracious and merciful is He that we can be on the brink of death, and He still doesn't turn His back on us, even when we've turned our backs on Him? Thankfully, in the end, she acknowledged God's presence and accepted Him as her Saviour.

Grace is often muted as a one-time event at the moment of salvation, but grace is an ongoing working out of our salvation, not stopping at the cross. We live in the resurrection power of what happens after the cross, when Jesus rose, leaving the grave clothes of death in the tomb. God's unmerited favour is upon us in these times. As we seek Him face to face, He desires that none should perish. Oh, what a marvellous God we worship!

Whether you've encountered the perfect love of God or not, I invite you to pray the following prayer with me:

God, I know you hear me, so I will speak to you and confess that I believe you are real. I am convinced that you can heal my broken heart, restore my life, and provide for every broken area of my life in miraculous ways. Today, God, as I acknowledge You and believe in You with all my heart, I give you total control to bring true transformation into my life, knowing and expecting that things will change. I pray this prayer in Jesus' Name. Amen.

Kingdom Keys

1. God's unmerited favour to you is grace. It's undeserved, and it cannot be earned. (John 3:16-17)

2. God is not slack, and He has promised that none shall perish but that all should come to repentance. (2 Peter 3:9)

3. Find someone trustworthy to work through the hard stuff with you and God.

***

2 Kings 4:8-37 tells the story of the Shunamite woman, who received a word from the Prophet Elisha and miraculously gave birth to a son. Elisha had seen her son's life from before he was born. As her son vibrantly grew, he became seriously unwell and died overnight. The prophet had a bed in the upper room of the woman's house, a place to rest when he passed by. After her son died, she placed the boy on the prophet's bed and, in faith, went out to find Elisha. She wasn't giving up on the promise that had come from the prophet's mouth. In desperation, she contended for her child's life.

After Elisha heard the news of the boy's death, he instructed his servant, Gehazi, to take his staff and place it on the face of the dead child. This demonstrates how the prophet delegated his authority. The people had expectations of prophets to move in miracles at that time. As ambassadors of God's voice and power, they could send others in their place with the same anointing and authority to do God's will. Such was the case with Gehazi.

Both Elisha and Gehazi totally expected this would raise the child from the dead, but it didn't work. No one could explain why Gehazi failed to resurrect the child. There are some speculations about his level of belief and faithfulness to the prophet he served, but we will never truly know. With the precedent of expectation and faith already set, Elisha then had to lay himself on the child. What a strange thing to do! Obviously, it's not up to us to decide how, where, or even why God heals; we just have to be ready when God calls. God moves in power where there is expectation.

***

God also knew this woman's heart was for her son to live. Since she had been caring for and nurturing His prophet by giving him a place to rest, He had given her the promise of a child. She showed the qualities of motherhood before becoming a mother because her heart was ready. She also knew he was a man of God and what that meant. If her household blessed him, she expected that God's presence would surely be in her home, along with the prophet.

I believe the times we're living in right now call for this type of faith and obedience in following God's instructions if we want to see people not just surviving but thriving in times of famine. Similar to the times of Old Testament prophets, today's climate of worshipping other gods and idols continues to rise. The time is coming when the economies of the world that have previously flourished will experience a lack. As God's people, we will watch Him miraculously provide despite the rumors of the land. Are you ready for that kind of faith to move through you?

Both Elijah and Elisha knew God was speaking and knew better than to get in the way. They may not have fully understood the instructions they gave these women, but they knew they had to declare the miraculous. These are the days we are still living in. Now is the time to speak up, unapologetically proclaiming the miraculous. A prophet's voice is not his own. That's what we must understand. We operate out of God's authority, not ours. We must speak what God says, with authority from heaven, with all of Him, and none of us.

4
Identity in Christ

And Mordecai told them to answer Esther: "Do not think in your heart that you will escape in the king's palace any more than all the other Jews. ESTHER 4:13

Our next story tells of one of God's most well-known, celebrated, and favoured women, Esther. If you're familiar with the story of Esther, I bet you've never considered her to be a desperate woman. Continuing with our theme, let's dive deeper into the Book of Esther and see what God wants to reveal.

In her desperate moments, Esther learned that knowing and adapting to the times is crucial. This woman interceded for her entire nation out of her obedience to God's call. Through her courageous perseverance amid trials and tribulation, Esther found favour with the king.

In summary, Esther prepared for years to meet the king in a way that ultimately won him over. Using strategies God revealed one step at a time, she won the battle for freedom for her entire nation (the Jewish people). The confidence of knowing her identity as a woman of faith motivated her, and after being crowned queen, she had the power and position to make a difference in the most crucial moment of her time.

As you continue reading here, I invite you to step into your identity as a child of God. Throughout this book, you'll receive impartations, discovering where you are to take a stand for righteousness in the spheres of influence God has placed you. Grab hold of them!

***

The Kingdom of God belongs to His children. The King, our Heavenly Father, our loving Papa God, is who He says He is. He's our Father, and as beloved Sons and Daughters of the King, we need to be secure in knowing that we are His children.

I'm grateful that I have felt loved all my life. My father's love for me was undeniable, and I was often called the apple of his eye. But I know not everyone has had the same loving experience as me. Some have felt that love sparingly, and some not at all.

As we journey through the story of Esther together, I want you to know that no matter who your earthly parents are, your Heavenly Father loves you. There's no room for doubt about that anymore. Whatever it takes, let the knowing of the Father's love settle in your heart.

One of the most important keys to the Kingdom of God is to know who you are. Getting your identity right is crucial from the get-go. Without your identity being solid inside, you will flounder, maybe even stumble, on your journey with the King. We have complete and total access to the throne room of God. We possess all the keys to the Kingdom, with free rein in every area. God does not hide or hold back anything from us who believe.

When we understand we're not visitors or slaves in the house of God but, by birthright (as born-again believers), Sons, and Daughters in the Kingdom, we can truly live from the safety of God's heart for us. We are indeed His cherished ones.

***

I have repeatedly seen that those engulfed in deep brokenness reap a glorious reward when they grasp their true identity in Him. People delivered from the dark bondage of despair, grief, and heartache often experience a miraculous sense of freedom. The moment of breaking out of the bondage of oppression of mental and physical pain is unmistakable in anyone's life. I have listened to people's stories of hopelessness, ruin, and rejection, who then found truth, love, and freedom. I have seen the transformative power of God's love at work in every corner of the world.

Just as God provided new coverings for Adam and Eve, Jesus Christ became our atonement, our new covering. When you, individually, encounter and accept that God loves you so much that He sent His only Son to set the world free from sin, you will transform from darkness to light. From sin to your original design through your relationship with God. You are perfect in your Father's eyes.

Freedom is your extraordinary inheritance as a child of God. It's worth so much more than any amount of gold! You become part of a global family, bringing comfort to the broken places of abandonment in the hearts of many. I have seen miraculous transformations, healings, and deliverances over many years, so I expect it will come to pass when God shows me something. Even if it has not happened yet, I believe. Once I have seen the outcome, I know, without a doubt, it is done!

***

I was nearly fifty years old when I discovered I was not who I thought I was all my life. At first, the news of my unknown identity was wrought with pain, an experience akin to so many orphans throughout the world. But through Esther's story and mine, I want to share the miraculous journey of becoming part of God's inheritance, His fantastic family.

I encourage you to recognize that these are more than just Bible stories. The Word of God is alive, meaning you can walk it out, just like I have, and Esther did. Esther, like me, wasn't who she thought she was at first. When her identity was revealed to her, she had to choose to accept it and step into it.

The Book of Esther contains the fullness of her story, but God wants you to know some specific things about identity. It starts with the understanding that Esther's uncle Mordecai raised her. Like Esther, my biological father did not raise me. However, I had a good man, like Mordecai, who took on the role of father. God spoke to me about Mordecai and his specific role in Esther's life—that he was a father to Esther, training her up in the way she should go. He became her spiritual father, in a sense. He became her father when she needed it the most.

Father figures are necessary in life. It's important to honour the Mordecai's, the dads who have stepped into a gap and become dads to many. I honour my earthly dad. And I honour my husband, who also stepped into the gap of father, raising my first two daughters as his own and in the way they should go. Men who follow God are essential in our lives as women. They are raising the next generation of Esthers that could save a nation.

***

When my identity was stripped from me, it created a deep inner turmoil in one sweeping moment. Thankfully, I had spiritual parents who provided a familiar space inwardly and outwardly that I could trust. I entered a mitzvah at their home, a bath used for ritual immersion (a Jewish traditional religious observation).

Following the Holy Spirit's guidance, I entered the mitzvah and submerged three times in a row. For the first submersion, I was on my back, and when I arose from the water, coughing and spluttering, Holy Spirit assured me I was okay and told me to go under face first next.

Going under again, I heard the word *clarity* and briefly opened my eyes beneath the water. I saw a yellowish-golden light opening like a portal before me, and for a moment, Jesus appeared as I held my breath. Before putting myself face first again for my third submersion, I told God I didn't want to leave without what I needed for the next season.

I wanted the miraculous, to see thousands of lives transformed! What I heard Him say was that it would be through writing. As I went under the water face first, He asked me to trust Him because He would breathe for me. I didn't hold my breath any longer. I opened my mouth and breathed under the water!

A woman's face emerged from the bottom of the bath, gazing up at me. I couldn't see the details of her face, but she had long brown hair and a brilliant diamond headdress. When I later searched online, I discovered the image I had seen was a crown for a Persian Princess. I saw a Royal Bride and heard from the Lord that she was being prepared.

***

The Holy Spirit spoke as I arose from the vision and the water. He told me that, like Esther, I was being positioned for such a time as this. That the miraculous would come forth in His presence, in His Glory. I was to stay in His presence and see His Glory come down and do it all. The Holy Spirit then instructed me to put my lips in the water—only my lips. He was cleansing them for the next season.

As I reflected on this supernatural experience, I realised the woman I saw in the water reflected me in the spirit. I also realised that, just like Esther, I was transitioning from the place of a daughter to a more royal position in the household of God's Kingdom. My life and position were shifting. He was preparing me for a royal position in His courts, the heavenly places—this was a new mantle of kingly authority and wisdom. Like Esther, I was born for such a time as this, for a position of power in the Kingdom of God.

From there, my instruction was simple: always remain humble-hearted and close to God, and never lose that first love of Jesus, who sacrificed everything so I may live. There is no greater love than this. The Holy Spirit is my inheritance, and the Spirit of the Lord lives in the Kingdom within me, just as it is for you.

God is so good at encouraging us and restoring our value when it feels stripped away by our enemies attempting to derail His plans. But stand firm, knowing that when God is for you, nothing can stand against you (Romans 8:31-34).

***

The enemy of my soul has targeted my identity throughout my life. But because of what I went through, identity is now where I have great spiritual authority as an overcomer. Growing up, I struggled with confusion and uncertainty. As an adult, I sought belonging, importance, and significance. The devil caused chaos in my life. Thank God, I now walk as a daughter of light, a light dweller, and a light bearer.

Family is the other area the enemy tried to destroy. He's good at pointing the finger at even the hardest of truths. Illegitimacy is a curse, and it was a curse for me that went backward and forward for several generations. But God breaks the curse of harlotry and covenants with false idols when true repentance occurs. The truth is that God's favour blesses widows and their children, as we saw in the earlier chapters.

Favour is your inheritance; heirs of grace are your inheritance. Titus 3 tells us to avoid foolish disputes, genealogy, contentions, and strivings about the law, for they are unprofitable. I reconciled that getting lost by trying to determine my earthly father's origins was a waste of my time.

Timothy says, "to speak evil of no one, be peaceable, gentle, showing all humility to all men, not by works of righteousness, but according to His mercy." Jesus saved us through the washing of regeneration and the renewing of the Holy Spirit. He poured Himself out abundantly. Having been justified by grace, we become heirs. Grace, mercy, and favour are inherently ours.

God's grace saved me, God's mercy set me free, and God's favour carried me through. I owe nothing to anyone. Christ paid and erased all my debts, including the debt of illegitimacy.

***

Once you settle your identity issues, you can move into your position of alignment and assignment with God and His people. Esther spent a year preparing to go before the king before he laid eyes on her, seven years after the pre-preparation to be equipped and ready for her mission.

While waiting, Mordecai gave her wise counsel, telling her not to reveal her family heritage. Mordecai was a man of the marketplace, keenly observing from the gates, always in the know about the political climate of his city. He always had Esther's best interests at the forefront of his mind.

Esther also received wise counsel from the king's trusted eunuch, Hegai, who carefully advised her on what jewellery to choose for her first moment before the king. She listened to both men's wisdom and, in doing so, gained favour. Godly wisdom often comes through trusted relationships of earthly means. God will guide you to the perfect place and position for His will.

In Esther 2:8-10, everything changed in her life instantaneously, and she yielded to it. She trusted God when the king's servant took her into his care. She left the comfort of her uncle's home and all that she had known. God removed her from the safety and protection of her uncle Mordecai and placed her in the custody and care of Hegai, whom the king had entrusted to her.

God also takes us into His custody and care. He has been preparing you and me because He chose us to be His royal representatives, just like Queen Esther. As the King's child, you are now being prepared for your next level of anointing and your next God assignment.

When King Ahasuerus was looking for a new queen, everyone heard his decree. That decree moved Esther from the outer courts to the inner courts of the palace. God's command, His decree, is what we respond to when we call to come into the inner courts of His Presence. In Esther 2:15-18, Esther received grace and favour in front of all who looked upon her. The king even made a celebratory feast for her, commanding everyone to arrive with gifts in Esther's name.

***

God walked me through the lessons in the Book of Esther over a period of nine months. During this time, I gained kingly favour. My position and wages increased, and then favour spilled out onto my entire household. God revealed something of Haman's rise in position as my position increased.

Haman was the king's right-hand man. In Esther 3, Haman receives a promotion that he doesn't really earn or deserve, but only because he has favour with the king. With an already tainted character, the power of his new position corrupted him even further.

In the king's kingdom, all the servants bowed down to Haman out of fear—except Mordecai. Haman's men hounded Mordecai daily. They tested Mordecai to see if his integrity would withstand the pressure. The power of corruption tried to rule over the kingdom, forcing itself daily upon the people it sought to oppress. It was a time of testing for God's people.

Haman knew of Mordecai's God and feared Him. Haman feared reprisal if he dared force Mordecai to obey, as he heard stories of the Jew's God and the consequences of attacking His people. May it be the same with us; we shall spread the Word of God to our enemies and instill a reverential fear in their hearts as we cling to the knowledge that He alone can create and destroy.

***

In Esther 3:8, Haman told King Ahasuerus there was a dispersed people group in the kingdom who didn't obey Ahasuerus's laws. Is this where we currently stand? Right now, God's people are spread out and dispersed among the nations, taking a stand against the ever-changing rules of the world's system. We are resisting evil rulers and their demands. Some, like Mordecai, have even stood up against our modern-day oppression of justice. For instance, we saw victory with the courts in America overturning Roe vs Wade. It takes courage and faith to take a stand for righteousness.

Taking it a step further, Haman sought a written order to destroy all Jews. The promise of money and greater riches gained the king's approval, but corruption and greed equal power and control—the world's system.

Haman and King Ahasuerus prepared, sealed, and published the document. They intended to kill, destroy, and steal from the Jewish people, so they sent out a decree for the complete eradication of all individuals, regardless of gender or age. They distributed a copy of the order as law in every province, mandating preparedness for that day. They released an edict of death over the Jewish people, essentially a nation. Haman deceived and tricked the King, but his ignorance made him complicit in the act, and his signature was the seal.

How many more times has this happened since then? Satan has repeatedly tried to wipe out God's people and has failed each time throughout history. In recent years, on a global scale, we saw laws change with rules, regulations, masks, vaccine requirements, passports, and much more.

During COVID-19, those in power sent edicts and decrees to break people's spirits. But if we don't succumb to death, we can become bringers of joy, hope, and love. Being God's mouthpiece in a time of despair means declaring the opposite, standing in truth, and, in doing so, believing that God will deliver us.

***

Haman devilishly devised a way to get the king to sign off on the decree being issued as law. The king handed over his people and finances to Haman with his signet ring to seal the order. He essentially gave the money and the people over to Haman to do with however he pleased. (Esther 3:11). Once Haman received the funds and the authority, he issued a decree of death that would wipe out an entire bloodline.

Doesn't that sound familiar? We see a similar decree in Exodus 1 when Pharaoh ordered all male children to be killed, attempting to wipe out the national bloodline of Jewish descent. John 10:10 states the intent of the evil one is to steal, kill, and destroy. The plan of Haman (Esther 4:7) involved the promise of payment. To make others rich, someone is always getting richer behind the scenes.

Mordecai then sent Esther the decree, as the palace was unaware of the situation beyond the gate. It reminds us that despite our closeness to God, we must stay aware of the world beyond our connection to Him. We want to avoid obliteration in ignorance.

Verse 11 highlights Esther's initial protest as she expresses concerns about being killed. As someone who hadn't been summoned into the King's presence by the King himself, this was a dire possibility.

Are you being called by your King into the place of intercession for your people, group, nation, or select area He has positioned you in? Are you being summoned to take up a new assignment, or are you called to take a stand at these times? Confirm the caller, the call, and your task. With confirmation, you'll finish your assignment with God's favour, unshakable and immovable.

***

In December 2021, God brought me a Korowai (Māori cloak/garment), a physical manifestation of a call I had received and had seen in the spirit nearly five years earlier. Called by my nation, I was bestowed a Korowai in the spirit at a church meeting. At that moment, an angel appeared and tied it in the front. It took time for me to receive it, however, with a complete understanding of the weight of accepting this call. It's an honour and commitment to carry this mantle.

The physical cloak has orange firebird feathers at the top, descending into blue and green, representing the eagle on the mountain and his view over the lakes and rivers. From a great height, a prophet's seat is in the heavenly places, observing the entire land. I knew God had called me for such a time as this!

As Esther received her royal garments and took up her position, she was adorned with a mantle and given authority. In Esther 6:8, King Ahasuerus summoned Esther and allowed her to make her requests known, promising to give her up to half the kingdom. Ask, and it shall be done. When we understand our identity and calling, we know we can petition our King, and He will give us access to the entire Kingdom if we humble ourselves to ask of Him (Matthew 7:7-8).

They also gave Esther the king's signet ring as a sign of authority and informed her she could write and issue a decree regarding the Jewish people to the entire kingdom. They explained to Esther that no one could revoke whatever she wrote in the king's name and sealed with his ring. So it is for us.

As believers in Christ Jesus, we have been granted all of heaven's authority. We have the King's signet ring of authority in what we both write and decree—an essential aspect of your identity. To grasp hold of it will change everything you do and say as a co-heir to Christ. This understanding will alter your position within the kingdom as you shift into knowing the power you have and begin to examine the integrity of which you distribute it.

***

As we approach the end of our study on Esther, consider that Chapter 9 discusses proper written word usage. When Esther went before the king, he commanded by written word (a letter) that Haman and his entire family would be hanged. This written command (9:26-27) led to the establishment of the two days of what is now known as Purim. Queen Esther wrote a second letter, establishing with full authority the details of Purim to be recorded for all the ages. Esther, a powerful woman, once an orphan, became a queen with royal authority, issuing decrees that saved a nation.

Mordecai also sent letters of peace and truth to confirm the days of Purim and their appointed time (9:30). Esther's decree, as written in a book, confirmed the matters of Purim, prescribing and decreeing, fasting, and lamenting. This celebration has lasted generations as a feast of freedom. They recorded all of this so that as you read it, you have a map to understanding your own God-given identity. Despite being an orphan, Esther was chosen, and she responded to the call.

***

Now, we fast-forward to Jesus' life. Although Jesus had Mary and Joseph as earthly parents, He knew his true identity. People found Him "going about His Father's business" and always "in His Father's house," but early in life, he learned ordinary carpentry skills from Joseph. His parents couldn't ignore or forget his miraculous birth, though. They knew he was both their son and the Son of God.

It was the same for me. God chose my earthly father, who sacrificed everything to become my dad and raise me. It cost him his life. His family turned their backs on him for many years as a result. And yet, he still made the choice. Mordecai chose to raise Esther, knowing something was on the way only he could prepare her for.

When you get tossed around and face challenges in life, your anchor amid the storm is knowing your identity as a child of God. Knowing that God loves you far beyond anything coming against you. Esther's firm belief in God and knowledge of being loved led to success in her quest. Nothing could stop her.

I pray for you to know that God has chosen you. That as you read these pages, you will embrace the fullness of who you truly are and see your identity in Christ. That it will be settled for you, once and for all. No more striving, no more seeking to belong, just a powerful knowing of the truth: God has chosen you for such a time as this.

Kingdom Keys

1. God has chosen you. (Isaiah 43:10)

2. You have been chosen for this moment in time. (Esther 4:14)

3. Your family name is God's name. You are His family. (Ephesians 3:15)

5
A Royal Inheritance

For this reason I bow my knees to the Father of our Lord Jesus Christ, from whom the whole family in heaven and earth is named. EPHESIANS 3:14-15

The world places a vital importance on inheritance. Sadly, many people don't know who their biological family members actually are. And when you don't know who your birth family is, you're left feeling devoid of any inheritance.

I grew up believing that I knew my genealogy and that the traits embedded within me were passed down from generation to generation. I spent years researching where our family had originated from with my grandfather. We traced the journey from England to New Zealand. And then, one day, it all meant nothing. It was all uprooted and gone.

The things that I had attributed to my personality were falsehoods. The revelation of that discovery was soul-crushing. When the devil wipes the floor with you, he does it with force and ferociousness. It's not just a light tap on the shoulder or a simple trip of your foot. Oh, no! It's total destruction, an assignment sent to wipe out your existence and all you know.

***

This sort of thing devastates people's minds and souls. The good news is God promises He is near to those who are broken-hearted and crushed in spirit (Psalm 34:18). Grief, rejection, abandonment, and betrayal come with a sense of lost inheritance. We struggle to rebuild what has been destroyed, putting our hope in the emergence of something better rising from the ashes.

Scripture tells us that as Jesus took off His garments and wrapped Himself in a towel to wash the disciples' feet, He laid aside His garments (John 13:4). I believe this expression enables us to see how the mantle of earthly inheritance can be laid aside for a Kingdom inheritance in Christ as we become co-heirs with Him.

As I laid aside my earthly mantle and walked in the inheritance of Christ, a myriad of changes ushered in. I felt a release from the issues that plagued me because of losing my earthly father's name. And with more persuasion and gentle encouragement from the Holy Spirit, I picked up my Heavenly Father's name.

John 13:12 says that after Jesus had washed all the disciples' feet, He put His garments back on. The putting on of His garments signifies the acceptance of the mantle of a Son or Daughter. As you take up your inheritance, you'll simultaneously step into the fullness of God's love and favour on your life. In humbling Himself, Christ gave us a living example of taking off the mantle of this world, a position of service, and placing on the mantle of God to live in the resurrection power of His grace, compassion, and mercy.

***

Jesus of Nazareth was the son of Mary and Joseph and the Son of God. He was a man, human in the flesh. God anointed Jesus with the Holy Spirit and power at the time of His baptism, and, as believers in Christ, we have both the Holy Spirit and power! We are to do all that Jesus did and more. You are to go about your communities, into all the world, doing good and healing all oppressed by the devil. Receive this as your invitation to take your metaphorical inheritance as part of God's family.

Don't believe the lies your mind tells you from lived experience. Believe in the truth that sets you free. My mind said that I had no family and did not belong anywhere. The truth is the total opposite of that lie.

By partnering with a lie, your soul will become downcast, and you will experience depression, which can lead to suicidal thoughts. If you've ever believed you're not worthy, don't belong, are not enough, or don't fit in, I want you to ask yourself when you first experienced that lie. Ask the Holy Spirit at what point you partnered with the lie. Then, ask what the truth is.

As you meditate on those three simple questions, you'll encounter freedom as the Holy Spirit begins to reveal and heal those broken places within. Don't condemn yourself, but allow Holy Spirit to convict you for transformation to take place (note convict, not condemn). Holy Spirit will guide you in truth. He's been waiting to redeem and set you free. He'll tell you things to come and reveal things He's already done. Holy Spirit speaks only that which He hears from the authority of the Father.

John 17:9 shows us that the Holy Spirit convicts those who do not believe so that they may believe. He convicts unrighteousness so that it may cease and righteousness may prevail.

***

I found the answers to the questions I had about my biological father by knowing that God is my loving Father. He's shown Himself real to me in this way. Throughout my life, I felt abandoned, alone, and unwanted, never quite fitting in. I wrestled with the genuine struggle of these feelings. After becoming a Christian, it only got worse. But as I grew as a disciple of Christ in my identity and authority, all the superficial layers melted away, and I had to get down to the root of the matter.

I thought I had a normal childhood by New Zealand standards. Not too bad, really. And for most of it, that's true. I was always a little odd, though. Imagine one of those kids with the curly, untamed hair that didn't look quite right in the lineup for school photos.

I was that quirky-looking kid with big, wide cat eyeglasses and no verbal filters, saying the most outlandish things at the wrong moment or in the wrong company. Impending doom lurked over me, always wondering if I was in trouble. I manipulated the truth on the defense until it became an outright lie. That was not my true identity, but in my brokenness, it was how I grew up from childhood into a young woman.

In John 18, Jesus prays to the Father for His disciples to be one with the Father, as He is. He prays that the love with which the Father loved Him may be in them and, in turn, in us. I prayed to God to resolve this within me once and for all. I asked Him to heal my orphaned heart and restore my love through His love. I asked Him to show me the blessings of Heaven's family in my life right then and there.

With that prayer, my whole countenance shifted. The love of God came upon me in new and rich ways as I accepted and received the love of the Father as my father. And all the lies of my lack of inheritance fell away. It was a difficult encounter to explain, but I knew my heart had been transformed, and I'd transitioned from salvation to inheritance. I now have my name secured forever.

***

Your inheritance is in all things. All things the Father has are also ours, and the Holy Spirit will tell us of it. John 6:13 says when the Spirit of Truth comes, He will guide you into all the truth. For He will not speak on His own, but He will speak whatever He hears. He will also declare to you what is to come. Just as God was with Jesus, God is also with us.

In John 3:2, Nicodemus, a Pharisee, went to Jesus, acknowledging who He was and declaring that no one could do the signs He was doing unless God was with them. John 8:29 reminds us that God sends us out to do His will. By doing His will, He is with us. The Father never leaves you alone as you go about pleasing Him through obedience.

By faith and grace, you and I have such a powerful inheritance! The Lord promises to grant us whatever we ask in the name of Jesus (John 16:23). What an amazing inheritance indeed! I cannot think of anything better! I picture my daughters asking their father for things, and He never denies them anything they need. God is much greater and a thousand times more able to answer and respond to us than our earthly fathers are, with mighty power, all we ask of Him. We need only ask.

Let us pray together now.

Father, I pray today knowing that you hear my prayer and with expectant faith that you will answer me. Restore my joy and the fullness of it. Set me free of all debts and burdens and increase in me favour with God and man, just as you did for Jesus (Luke 2:42). Increase your inheritance in me in every area of life so I may be a greater blessing to others. Thank you for my inheritance of joy, faith, and great love. In Jesus' name. Amen.

Kingdom Keys

1. There is no reason to fear; God is with me. (Isaiah 41:10)

2. The Lord will perfect that which concerns me. (Psalm 138:8)

3. I will dwell safely in my home; God will protect me, and I will know how much He cares for me. (Ezekiel 28:26)

4. My God will supply all my needs according to the riches of His Glory in Christ Jesus. (Philippians 4:7)

5. I have new expectations according to God's truth.

6. I am accepted, not rejected.

7. I have good, loyal, faithful relationships.

8. I do not have to fight for my position. My position is secure in God's house. I am loved and well-positioned in God's Family.

9. I have a seat at My Father's Table, and there is more than enough room. I flourish in His courts with thanksgiving and praise.

***

The anointing is the Father's blessing. God instructed the Prophet Samuel to anoint Saul and make Him king. God has chosen you to receive His blessing, too, the fullness of His love in your life. Our Father knows the desires of His children's hearts, and He delights in fulfilling them.

1 Samuel discusses Hannah's life and God's faithfulness in fulfilling her desires through healing and deliverance. Hannah poured out her heart to God, but not by praying out loud. Her desperate desire to be a mother spoke to God of her pain and suffering.

What I love about Hannah's story the most is that after all she goes through, she receives her miracle: the child she longed for. Like Hannah, my firstborn as a new believer in Christ was also miraculous. He was born despite the evil reports saying I couldn't have more children without dying. He was delivered by c-section in the breach position with the cord around his neck three times, defying all the odds!

I became a mother early in life and wasn't all that successful. So, when God redeemed my life, giving me a second chance to be a mother, I embraced the blessing with total gusto. I became the ultimate Christian mother! Raising this new creation surrounded by Veggie Tales books, daily scripture readings, Hillsong Kids dance, and worship videos, I was determined to do better!

***

Hannah had to give her son Samuel away, though. Just as Mary released Jesus, Hannah released Samuel. Both gave their children back to God despite suffering through their surrender. Hannah promised God she would dedicate Samuel to Him, and she gave him back to God at a determined time. After weaning him, she entrusted Samuel to the priests so they could teach and train him in the ways of God. He was young, and my heart ached as I read this story. I understood how terribly hard it must have been to give him up.

Hannah's story makes me think of my son, Shaun. Shaun's name in Gaelic means "God's gift or God is gracious," which perfectly reflects his spirit and personality. He was such a gentle and loving soul; having him was God's gift, not just to me and our family but to the world. I've come to realise our children are not ours. They belong to us briefly. And although God had chosen me to be this boy's mother, He was ultimately God's son.

While we journeyed through the trials of adolescence, I prayed for the strength to surrender my son to the Father. With time, as God watched and trained Shaun, He would fulfil the good work within him. I thanked God for giving us Shaun. He loved our son more than I could ever love him.

I began to understand that I could release Shaun back into His care, just as Mary and Hannah had done with their sons. I found reassurance in knowing God would shower His favour upon him, as He did Jesus and Samuel. But I didn't recognise how vital this revelation of trusting God with my heart, my son, would be.

Hannah's son, Samuel, had the heart of a deliverer, growing up to become a Seer Prophet in his nation. Had his mother not allowed him the space and freedom to go, he may never have become the person he was meant to be. We all have dreams for our children, but trusting God with His dream for them is something we can step into with total confidence as mothers in Christ. We can trust God with our children. With the plans and hopes He has for them today.

Kingdom Keys

1. Do as God says in His word. He will reveal things for you to do.

2. Serve Him obediently.

3. Trust Him wholeheartedly.

4. Release your children to God for His will to be done through them on earth as it is in Heaven.

6

New Miracles

So Jesus said to him, "Unless you see signs and wonders you will not believe." JOHN 4:48

We decided it was time to sell our house. I also decided to tell the realtor about my unique approach to property sales. As I shared my faith walk with him, he opened up to me about his mother, a mighty prayer warrior, and his sister fighting blood cancer.

At that moment, the Holy Spirit impressed upon me that I was hosting God's presence and reminded me that I have God's anointing to heal and cast out demons. So, I asked if I could pray for his sister. He agreed, saying he would try anything. We prayed then and there, and I committed to praying for her continually.

Later, I spoke with my local church prayer team, helping raise the collective faith for this woman's healing. As we came into agreement, in unity, we anointed a scarf with oil and prayed over it. Believing that our prayers were sealed with the blood of Jesus, we gave the scarf to the realtor to send to his sister. This was done with the intention that our faith would be released to her as soon as she came into contact with the garment.

***

Acts 19:11-12 establishes the biblical precedent for this type of transference, where handkerchiefs that Paul had touched were taken to the sick, causing diseases and evil spirits to leave them—this proves that items can carry the anointing. Transference is possible when a person cannot be there; in the same way, Jesus is no longer physically with us, but His anointing is. You and I can do this, too; we can pray and anoint a cloth to send in our place.

The realtor wept as he stood with us for his sister's healing. Being in one accord is essential because people often ask for help without real expectations of the outcome. However, we saw the woman of Sidon, without faith, access the miraculous through the obedience of a prophet. So, if He did it for her, He will do it again. Anything is possible with God!

A few weeks later, the realtor came back to me with great excitement, telling me that the death sentence over his sister had shifted. She was in remission! The specialists even changed her diagnosis from six months to live to at least another four to five years. From death to life! We continue to declare the fullness of this healing. To this day, she lives with her young children. They get to have their mother! Praise God! This was the beginning of the first of new miracles!

***

The first miracle Jesus performed was turning water into wine at a wedding feast in John 2. Those in attendance got to be first-hand witnesses of the principles of the Kingdom. Water into wine equals plain into extraordinary! They may have been seated at a wedding banquet with the King, but they didn't know it at first. In the same way, we don't always realise we have unmerited access to the Kingdom and all within it until we encounter Jesus or one of His miracles.

At a wedding feast in Jewish culture, the host always starts by serving the best wine first. As the feast progresses and people get increasingly drunk, they will pour lesser-quality wine because they're less apt to notice the quality. However, in the case of Jesus' first public miracle, the opposite happened. The guests must have thought the host saved the best wine for last because it was so good. Not only was it exceptionally good, but it was a great honour for them to receive such fine wine at a later hour. Isn't this what God does? He saves the best for last!

***

How did this miracle come to pass, though? Basically, through a wedding party drinking so much wine, they ran out! Jesus even said it was not yet His appointed time for public ministry, but His mother, Mary, insisted He fix the situation. It's important to note that Mary was highly concerned that running out of wine would put the host to shame. Why should we take note of this? Because it wasn't her wedding or even her problem. Why would she even care? Simple. Because the family of God is not concerned with self. It's concerned with others.

Although it wasn't Mary's responsibility, she put others above herself. Perhaps she was concerned that people would talk poorly about the hosts, as running out of wine might suggest that the bridal party didn't care about their guests. Her concern was for reputation, it would seem. But Jesus quickly rebuked her concerns (John 2:4). He wasn't worried about reputation, gossip, or what people might think or say. And if you do just as the servants did, obeying Jesus in your own life, then you shouldn't be concerned about reputation, either.

Jesus loved His mother and how she cared for the wedding party and the guests. He didn't want her in distress. It's the same love and compassion we experience when we move in His Spirit for others. Although the realtor's sister, the woman with blood cancer, had no connection with me, it was her brother's love for her that moved the compassion of Christ in me to see her healed. His love compelled me to send the prayer scarf, believing in her healing.

John 2:5 says that Mary told the servants to do whatever Jesus asked. We are also called to do what Jesus asks of us, no matter the cost. Ultimately, the servants knew precisely where the new wine came from—Jesus. And He knew they would spread the word of this miracle, stepping out publicly in faith. Now it's your turn! Go out and spread the good news!

***

The invitation of God is to partake of Christ and walk in the fullness of your identity as a believer, full of His love and doing the will of the Father, just as Jesus did. The Father's authority is the Word. Scripture describes Jesus as the Word in the flesh, and His words are full of mercy and grace. When we believe, healing will occur.

The story of the nobleman's son in John 4:46-54 is another example of this. Once again, we find another desperate parent looking for answers for his sick child. This man's faith was so big that he believed Jesus's words of healing for his son from a distance. He then went home and found him well and alive. Jesus didn't ask or pray to the Father. He pronounced it so, and it was done. "Your son lives" (John 4:50). Jesus never physically touched the boy, just as I never came into contact with the woman with the blood cancer.

When we understand the power of our decree, we see the manifestation of our words. Often, I see the end of a thing before its beginning. What does that mean? Simply put, when I declare something is done, whether or not I have seen the physical evidence, it is done. I expect the miraculous because I know my God, my identity, and the authority with which I speak.

***

Jesus' first sign of the miraculous was turning water into wine. He performed a physical miracle, changing particles, atoms, and structures of one thing into another. This displayed heavenly science at work, the miracle of transforming molecular structure. If Jesus could turn water into wine and see the change of a physical element in one moment, then by His decrees, it's the same for the molecular structure of the body. Every virus and disease we encounter today is subject to the Word of God. Freedom from disease is possible for those who believe.

A man in John 5 was bound to illness for 38 years, leaving him unable to move. Jesus approached the paralytic one day and asked him if he desired to be healed. Despite responding with a barrage of excuses, Christ knew he desperately wanted to be made well. And that he was. Christ healed him of a lifetime of affliction; he quite literally stood up and walked forward into his destiny and purpose.

As the man walked free, the religious naysayers criticised Jesus for healing him on the Sabbath, a day of rest. The Pharisees called it work, making it illegal and sinful. They were so caught up in accusations that they didn't even marvel at the miracle. Their focus was on finding fault. Be on guard as you step out in faith and walk in the miraculous; there will always be mockery and ridicule from those wanting to find fault. Don't get offended. The power you wield is not your own. It belongs to God, and He is your Great Defender.

The woman with the blood issue in Mark 5 and the paralytic both suffered chronic physical ailments and were miraculously healed in an instant. This is akin to the widow woman at the beginning of this book, who knew and experienced God's compassion through His prophet on earth, who healed her through her faith amid her desperation. Healing miracles are found throughout the Old and New Testaments.

***

As we continue in John 5, we see Jesus following up with the paralytic man. He gave the man a generous gift of healing, but Jesus wasn't finished with him yet. In the temple court in John 5:14, He sternly warned the man to stop sinning or something worse would happen to him.

Even the most miraculous healings can be taken away if a person continues in their sinful ways. We all have free will. Healing isn't just a gift. It's for showing the power and glory of God and bringing people to salvation. Remember that.

Jesus healed the paralytic man first, but knowing he also needed transformation of the soul, He returned to him, addressing his sin. Jesus did the opposite with the woman at the well. He first healed her soul and then gave her eternal life. When we look at the woman with the issue of blood, her supernatural faith in Jesus ultimately brings her instantaneous healing. And then we remember the widow at the beginning of this book. She received deliverance and freedom but needed more time and miracles to trust God fully.

There is no remedy, programme, method, or pattern to adhere to other than following Christ. We must love people just as God loves people. He met them with love, seeing and knowing their needs, just as He sees and knows each of our needs. I pray as this chapter comes to a close, your heart will flood with love and compassion. That you come to understand the joy of the Lord is the fuel you need to keep going in the times we are living in. This is your invitation to the miraculous. To quote CS Lewis, "Joy is the serious business of heaven."

The result of healing the paralytic man was Jesus being further harassed, and attacks began forming against Him, citing He was claiming equality with God. Be warned and expect that this too can happen to you. Don't be distracted by it. Jesus tried to explain that He didn't act on His own authority but on the authority of God. We also have the same power and authority to bring death to life through Jesus Christ.

Let us pray together now:

Father, I believe your anointing is on me. I am weak, but you are strong and mighty. Your Spirit is in me. The same Dunamis power that lives in Christ Jesus lives in me. I can do all things through Christ in me. It is no longer me who lives but Christ who lives in me. I thank you, Holy Spirit, that as I speak, your words will go out in power, and I will see healing in people's lives. Amen.

Kingdom Keys

1. Faith—You have it. Exercise it.

2. Holiness—Maintain your relationship with the Father and only do, say, and speak what He directs.

3. Pure Heart—Have clean hands and clean Lips.

4. Repent—There will be hard days, but remember, God forgives.

7
The Father's Table

The Lord is my shepherd; I shall not want. PSALM 23:1

Once you have your identity sorted, it's time to sit at the Father's table and inspect all that's laid before you. The table symbolises many things. Let's discuss the guests and the invitation to take a seat. We must understand the fullness of our God-given identity and the miraculous power of God working through us. As sons and daughters, we all have a seat at the table. The Father's table is our access point.

Let's consider the promises offered In Psalm 23. God first establishes His authority and purpose for us. God is the Shepherd. It's His job, if you like, to take care of us, and He does it well. Verse 1: "I shall not want." I need nothing because He provides everything for me. Then verses 2 and 3 describe God creating us to live in the soul realm, at peace and still. "He leads us in paths of righteousness for His Name's sake." He guides us toward salvation.

Psalm 23 teaches us that we cannot avoid trouble and hard times. We may experience deep grief or come close to death, but we get through these seasons by simultaneously walking in confidence, knowing God promises to be with us, always. His rod and staff represent the authority that will continuously carry us through.

God says He's prepared a table before us in the presence of our enemies. We have the victory, and He has anointed us with oil. Our cup is described as running over, signifying we have every blessing: this is symbolic of the cup Jesus used at the Last Supper. He tells us to remember Him as we drink from it, the cup of victory.

The last promise of Psalm 23 assures us that goodness and mercy will follow us all the days of our lives. Can it get any better than that?! Our eternal promise is that we can dwell in the house of the Lord forever, and that's exciting!

***

This one psalm reveals that the family table is fully laden and never runs out. Embrace your birthright and stand confidently in this inheritance, knowing your power and authority. Let's cling to this amidst upcoming economic predictions. There may be predictions of lack in the world, but there's no lack for those who believe! We can partake of the overflow of blessings at the King's table. God's table overcomes worldly enemies. He prepares the table; the feast of blessings is before us, and the devil can't touch it.

We must see and understand this picture. The devil cannot enter! Being in the presence of our enemies means they can stand and watch as we feast. My enemies being at the table is of no consequence! God's power is greater than those watching and cursing. The sooner you grasp this revelation as your reality, the sooner you'll see an upgrade in your realm of authority.

The family table from your house to my house may look a little different, but the structure of the Father's table from a heavenly realm has core values that are universal throughout the Kingdom of God. You are sons and daughters of Light.

In the book of John, Jesus says, "Those who walk in darkness are of darkness and cannot understand. Those who walk in light are the world's light, carrying His light." 1 John 4:4 speaks of how you have overcome evil spirits because He who is in you is greater than he who is in the world. Taking your rightful seat at the Father's table, grab hold of this truth today.

Let's pray:

God, I thank you for taking care of every need I have. Thank you for magnifying your goodness all around me. I am blessed to be a blessing to others in this world so that my generosity may show the Glory of God. Father, thank you for showering me with generosity. May it increase, not because of me, but because of You. Thank you for Your financial blessings, allowing me to testify to even more of your goodness and enabling me to help others. Amen.

Kingdom Keys

1. Love is essential and non-negotiable at the table.

2. We all bring something unique to the table. Your seat is valuable, and so are you.

3. We sit together and share from all the table. God's resources are endless.

4. There's always company at the table. You are never alone.

***

What we proclaim with our mouths manifests from heaven to earth, establishing reality as we speak. Therefore, we must watch our words! You're not just a guest at the table. You're a family member by covenant and by name.

When you establish your newborn identity and speak it forth, you are now a child of God Almighty, the Sovereign King and Creator of everything. You're a co-heir with Christ, seated in heavenly places with the Holy Spirit operating in and through you in the earthly realms.

You know that wonderful feeling of returning home after you've been away for a while? It's like you can fully relax and just be yourself again. I experienced something similar when I returned to my cultural roots on a trip to the North Island of New Zealand. I was able to be myself and discover more of my roots.

A woman who accompanied me on that trip watched me closely, describing a moment when she could see I was very connected with God. With my feet firmly planted on the seabed while the water raged over me, it was as if I had my Turangawaewae back and found my sense of belonging. As someone who hadn't had a great home life growing up, with no church life until I met Jesus at a movie theatre in my early thirties, it seemed freedom at its finest.

***

I wrote my first book on the stories of three women from the Bible that God had highlighted to me. Each one resonated with my life, and I wove reflections of them around me for the reader to relate to. However, when I encountered Joseph's story, I realised that although I had read it countless times before, now I could also see myself in him! What a revelation. The Word really is living, and we are alive in it!

I understood Joseph's dreams and how he innocently wanted to share with utter excitement what God had shown him. And yet, people severely rejected and hated him for it. Like Joseph, I, too, had gone into a pit. Although nobody sold me into slavery or imprisoned me, it felt like the church rejected, abused, and abandoned me in my time of need. Rather than rallying family around to help me understand the gifts God gave me, they shunned and divorced what I carried on their assumptions.

God brought restoration and took me to a place of identity and authority that was always mine for the taking. Like Joseph, I triumphed over struggles and emerged stronger. I returned to this church as an act of reconciliation and witnessed God's divine restoration during my first sermon. In the weeks prior, the church's pastor had preached the story of Joseph. As I shared my testimony of Joseph's story, I realised it was not a coincidence I was there.

***

Ephesians 4:1-3 discusses how we are to live out our Christianity. We are to walk worthy of the calling to which we are called. We are to endeavour to keep the unity of the Spirit in the bond of peace. This peace is a Kingdom key.

Being a disciple of Christ, we aim to become more Christlike, knowing our spirit is already in Christ. We should have fellowship with one another in love, just as Christ loves us. We must diligently work to maintain the unity of the Spirit, which brings us together in peaceful harmony.

The Spirit's unity differs from believers' unity as individuals. The unity of you, the Father, the Son, and the Holy Spirit is most important. Our spirits, originating from God, should also not have any discord between them. Therefore, you must remain close to God and in right relationship with Jesus and the Holy Spirit.

What creates disunity is our personalities, the soul of man. There can be no disunity at the Father's table. A murderous heart cannot contain the Glory of God (Matthew 5:2-25). In Matthew 5, Jesus speaks of what it is to have a murderous heart. You may not believe it applies to you. *Not me, never! I'm not a murderer!* But Jesus redefines our way of thinking about murder. He submits that murder comes when we nurse anger against our brother. Calling someone good for nothing is having an opinion of their worth. Calling someone a fool warrants the severest condemnation—eternal damnation in hell.

***

Joseph's brothers were jealous of his gift and favour with their father. He did nothing to cause or create the jealousy. It simply arose in them. I've often seen envy and comparison be the downfall of those truly in love with Jesus. To their demise, they place importance on their positioning. Let me be transparent and say that I, too, can fail in these areas. Only through true repentance, prayer, and leading from the Holy Spirit that God has redeemed my relationships through His grace.

Jesus gives us a warning and offers eternal wisdom in Matthew 5:25: "If someone sues you, come to terms with him quickly, while you and he are on the way to court; or he may hand you over to the judge, and the judge to the officer of the court and you may be thrown in jail!"

So today, let us recognise we should quickly resolve our issues with one another and come to a resolution before we reach the court outside God's throne room, lest someone hands us over for judgment. Let us recognise and celebrate our differences as unique creations rather than becoming jealous or competitive. Let us run the race set before us with joy in the abilities and talents God has bestowed upon us.

I pray for you and me to see reconciliation and restoration through God's Word come to pass in all areas of our lives, including our families, relationships, workplaces, and the Kingdom of God.

Declare with me:

I am freed and forgiven. My past no longer defines me. I no longer walk in the shadow of lies and shame. I receive forgiveness and freedom, and now shame no longer defines me. Just as I have made mistakes, my children also make mistakes. But forgiveness and freedom are also given to them, freeing them from the captivity of shame. We are Family, no longer bound by the accuser's shame. I walk in dignity and humility as a risen one, and with a healed heart, I will keep moving forward, no longer broken-hearted or bound but completely reconciled, restored, and free!

***

Are you not a tent maker? Are you not a carpenter? Are you not called to sustain life by working instead of begging for it? God has not created us to beg for money to do the work He intends for us to do. And not everyone who comes into the Kingdom of God is called to lead a church or only work and serve within the walls of one. They're not the only ones invited to the Father's table. A whole world out there needs us to bring Christ to them daily. That means we must be in the world!

God's house is not a business; it's a family. Jesus being about the Father's business didn't mean He was turning the gospel into a business venture. He was doing the Father's will with power and authority. Jesus was so disturbed by business operations within the synagogues that He flipped over the moneychangers and merchants' tables, creating a whole messy scene (Matthew 21:12-17). God created us metaphorical tent makers and carpenters for a reason, so we would be involved in the day-to-day activities of mankind and have endless opportunities to speak Jesus into the lives of the lost. Even many of the teachers and rabbis in biblical times sustained their families through an income aside from teaching.

Perhaps it's a question for you to be asking God. Ask Him how you are to sustain life on earth. In what way does He want you to provide for your family *and* the Kingdom family? When you sit at the Father's table, the provision is there. But in daily living, we often misunderstand what partaking of that table should be like. Christians have manufactured a mystical element in their faith, where money suddenly appears. Don't get me wrong; I've witnessed firsthand God touching bank accounts with the provision and miraculous provision at that! He's certainly not above miraculously providing funds when there appear to be none.

Know this—there is never a provision without a purpose. But we must use wisdom to get by in the world. As a daughter of the Most High, I always ask my Father how He would like me to use the skills and abilities He has attributed to my life.

***

Before creation, God determined what your life should look like. It's a process. However, here I am in my fifties, growing, maturing, and understanding that becoming a disciple of Jesus means I'm not limited to serving within church walls to be serving in the Kingdom of God. Serving the Family takes place everywhere, and at all times, serving mankind is the work of our hands. Dear friend, I encourage you to lay your God-given talents at the foot of the cross. As you surrender your talents, ask the Lord if He would have you pick them back up and what that looks like.

How is it that your life can bring joy to others? My life's purpose is to bring hope and healing to the nations. The working out of that is in God's hands and looks differently each day. And the good news is that it can look like anything! There's no limit. There's no one lane.

Some days, I'm creative. On other days, I'm using my administrative gifts. There are days when it's through a kind word or a hug. Or, it's a call to write the stories of God woven in amongst the stories of real-life moments. To share those stories with the world so they, too, may know the goodness and glory of our God. Take the limits off! Prepare for a new thing to spring forth with fresh revelations as these Kingdom keys become your reality.

The Spirit of the Lord God is upon Me, because the Lord hath anointed Me to preach good tidings unto the meek. He hath sent me to bind up the broken-hearted, to proclaim liberty to the captives, and the opening of the prison to them that are bound.
ISAIAH 61:1 NKJV

Kingdom Keys

1. There's room for all at the Father's table.

2. I have my unique position and do not need to compete.

3. God has created me for good works so I will work to the best of His ability within me.

8

Greater Authority

Confess your trespasses to one another, and pray for one another, that you may be healed. The effective, fervent prayer of a righteous man avails much. JAMES 5:16

Let's complete our journey of equipping with a final area of greater authority. I preached in a small church in Galt, USA, a few years back. I spoke about how I became a desperate mother when my son got involved in some unsavoury things at one point. My heart for my son became full of God's love as I warred for the promises of his life to come forth. I shared how I pressed harder on the altar to receive the oil I needed from the Lord. As a result, I witnessed a breakthrough as my son received deliverance from oppression.

Don't underestimate love. It exudes an incredible power that's impossible to deny. Just like Jairus went to Jesus (Mark 5:23) for his daughter's healing, we can also intercede on our children's behalf. We don't need their permission. Regardless of age, pray to God for their genuine and necessary needs. The effective, fervent prayer of a righteous man or woman avails much.

***

Jairus, a wealthy and respected man, served as a ruler of the synagogue and could undoubtedly afford any doctor and treatment. In desperation, though, he ran to Jesus for help, even when other religious leaders were available. Through that act, it was his faith that gained God's favour. He begged the Lord, asking Him to lay hands on his little daughter, on the brink of death, so that she could live. Jairus had faith that Jesus would heal his daughter. He knew he could go on her behalf.

I had become that desperate parent like Jairus, feeling in my spirit that my son was getting close to death, unaware of all he had gotten mixed up in, but knowing I had to war for his life. Jesus was the only one who could protect him from harm. Trust your knower regarding your family members, especially if you are a praying parent!

In terms of earthy ability, Jairus had much, but he knew nothing mattered as his daughter's life was hanging in the balance. He ran and searched for the one he had faith in—Jesus! But Jesus couldn't immediately leave because he was attending to the woman with the issue of blood. When Jesus eventually arrived at the house, they declared the child was dead.

As other individuals arrived, they told Jairus his daughter was dead and to not trouble the Teacher any further (Mark 5:35). Upon hearing the spoken word, Jesus comforted Jairus, urging him not to be afraid and to ignore the voices speaking death over his child. He urged him to listen to His life-affirming voice instead. Hold on to your faith and believe!

***

The same had occurred in my son's life. Many lacked my supernatural faith. I needed to push aside all the voices around me, standing firm in agreement with Christ for Shaun's deliverance and healing. Jesus saved him from near death during that time, as I clung on for his dear life.

When Jesus entered Jairus' house, He asked why they were making such a commotion and weeping. He declared the child was not dead but sleeping (Mark 5:39-40). Of course, they ridiculed Him, so Jesus put them all outside. With the disciples and the child's parents, He entered where the child lay. Note that even those inside of Jairus' home declared his daughter dead. Your immediate family may not have the faith you hold, but Jesus does, and He is standing with you.

Jesus kicked everyone else out and brought the parents into agreement with Him. As you partner with Christ in faith for your children, He'll enter that situation, and you'll see your children raised up again. Jesus recognises parental authority and acknowledges parental authority. We, too, should contend for our children. Amen!

> *Most assuredly, I say to you, the Son can do nothing of Himself, but what He sees the Father do; for whatever He does, the Son also does in like manner. For the Father loves the Son and shows Him all things that He Himself does; and He will show Him greater works than these that you may marvel. For as the Father raises the dead and gives life to them, even so the Son gives life to whom He will. JOHN 5:19-21*

***

Back at the American church, I noticed a woman kindly pushing her husband forward for prayer after I shared the message about being in desperate places. A man and his wife stood before me, full of hope for a breakthrough. This time, the Lord gave me the word *unspeakable things*. I heard James 5:16 in my spirit, and the Holy Spirit instructed me to request that the man confess the *unspeakable things*.

Now, this is when you know you're operating in God's authority. There's no way that idea was mine. I just moved in total obedience because I know the voice of the Holy Spirit and trust in His ways, which are higher than mine. No matter how weird or odd it may seem or feel, we go with the flow, trusting God. Right?!

Bringing dead hearts back to life is certainly not an effortless task. As this man confessed, he revealed a very personal situation from his childhood that now affects his marriage and relationship with God. His stepfather had beaten and treated him poorly. His mother had not stepped in on his behalf due to her genuinely unfavorable circumstances.

He quietly confessed to me the unspeakable things that had taken place, and his countenance grew lighter as he did. He poured out his heart, surprising his wife with things she'd never heard. As the burdens lifted, shame also lifted. He said he felt lighter, so we declared James 5:16 over him. I then called him and his wife to anoint and proclaim a marriage blessing over them with their pastors.

The mother's heart for this man poured from me as I heard his confession. The Father's love saw him healed and restored. I poured out my little oil, and it multiplied abundantly. We can stand in the gap with parental authority, spiritually and physically, for our children and the children of God.

I followed up with the pastors of that church, and they told me the couple was doing amazing. The husband had returned to church, serving God and his family like never before. That's what freedom from oppression looks like! That's what happens when dead hearts begin to beat!

Mark 16:20 says that when we preach the Word, God will confirm it, working through us miraculously. But we must know our authority to see those transformative miracles flow at greater levels. God's Word set this couple free, not my words. There's a big difference. The Word is authoritative; you hold that authority every time you speak.

***

Another time, I was at a meeting in the Los Angeles area. It brought me great joy to have been invited by a mentee to her healing worship event. However, the pastor of the event had limited supernatural experiences and wasn't sure how my presence would impact the ministry's appearance. Unconcerned ourselves, we carried on as God gave us a powerful word.

The pastor urged anyone needing prayer to step forward. Several people answered. The pastor's wife approached me with a woman. Before agreeing to pray, I requested the pastor first grant me authority. He came, and together, they blessed and released me to pray as a house leader would.

Over the years, I've learned the hard way about territorial spirits. There's great significance in freely ministering with authority. Everyone must obey authority. My history of abuse by authority figures has helped me understand this. Getting to my current place of confidence and certainty was an arduous journey.

As I prayed for the woman, I got the same word again—*unspeakable things*. Continuing to move with the Holy Spirit, I asked her several questions. She shared how men in the workplace had literally hunted her down and accused her of inappropriate dress and behaviour, causing her to be on the brink of losing her job. She confessed she was also in yet another abusive relationship after her marriage ended.

She had lost other jobs when people accused her of being sexual towards coworkers, and she felt she was not being listened to despite having done nothing wrong. When we met, there was nothing about her that showed any outward, overt sexuality. About to lose everything: her home, land, and finances, the woman recognised this was becoming a pattern in her life.

I suddenly saw a magazine on a table in the spirit. I shared what I was seeing, and she suddenly began manifesting as she confessed her addiction to pornography. Upon this demonic exposure, we prayed and saw her delivered from a spirit of pornography that bound her for years. Her pastors were surprised but handled it beautifully with great care and love.

Months later, someone told me that the woman had left the abusive relationship she was in and her job because of sexual harassment charges, but she was now successfully rebuilding her life. She was healing and being made whole with pastoral support.

***

The following weekend, when I returned home to New Zealand, a man from another church approached me for prayer, and once again, the Holy Spirit revealed the same message—unspeakable things. Since God had shown Himself in America, I knew what I needed to do.

I briefly shared the testimony from the previous weekend as the young man stood before me, crying. His wife accompanied him, and I kindly asked her to step away. I could see him in the spirit, curling up inside into a foetal position every time she rubbed his back, and I knew he needed space from her to let this all out.

Once we were alone, he confessed what he was hiding. As I prayed and saw God set him free, according to His word (James 5:16), the man left his shame at the door and walked out a new creation in Christ. His wife contacted me later, telling me how her husband had gone home and confessed everything to her. It turns out she also had much to confess. They prayed together about all of it.

I'm so happy to testify they are now an amazing couple serving God with all their hearts. Their marriage is blessed because they were both set free!

Kingdom Keys

1. When you know your authority, God moves in power.

2. Tune in to the Holy Spirit, listen well, and be obedient.

3. You will have to contend for the promises of God and hold firm to His word.

4. Love is the overcoming power of God.

When Jesus heard it, He marveled, and said to those who followed, "Assuredly, I say to you, I have not found such great faith, not even in Israel!" MARK 8:10 NKJ

***

Authority is the believer's key to seeing heaven manifest on all the earth. Even people during Jesus' time acknowledged His authority, including oppressors and those who opposed Him. That's why they also feared Him. Christians sadly spend too much time empowering the devil and giving him undue credit for things he has no authority over. And once you give him the credit, he moves in like a flood.

I've heard the same story with varying details one too many times. For example, someone may be heading to an important meeting when their tire suddenly blows out. They declare that it's all-out warfare and the devil is attacking them. Is that *really* the case?

Now, hear me. Attacks of these kinds happen, for sure. However, most of the time, I ask if you have checked your tire pressure recently. Are your tires bald? Did you hit something while driving? Perhaps because your tires have a weak point, they merely blew out. Before attributing it to the devil, my husband often asks people if they ever pause, taking a moment to consider it might just be life.

The devil knows Jesus' power and authority. When you walk into a room and people shake and manifest or start taking offense to things you never even said, it's not your power they're contending with. That, my friends, is purely the power of Christ in you ministering to them. You carry God's presence, and everything in creation knows it! Do you?

In Matthew 8, Jesus tells a story where a Roman centurion goes to Him seeking healing for his servant. First, we note that the centurion from the oppressors' camp went directly to Jesus. He didn't summon Jesus or bring him before him, which he could've done. No, he went to Him because he knows who he's dealing with. The oppressor went to Christ for help! Take note! Recognise your authority!

The next point of authority the centurion recognised was that the word of Christ was all he needed. Jesus stayed where he was, spoke, and healed the servant. The devil, mankind's greatest oppressor, surpasses even the centurion. The devil knows what it means to have Jesus living inside of you. He's very aware of who you are and what you carry! For millennia, the devil has aimed to deceive and outsmart Christ's followers, making them believe the enemy holds greater power. And he's still trying to deceive. However, the devil can't accomplish anything unless we allow him to.

When we don't recognise our position, we're effectively just handing over our power. Knowing who we are, what we carry, and whose authority we walk in allows us to enter a realm of new knowledge. Jesus marvelled at the centurion's faith, and as He spoke, the centurion's servant received healing by His word. Faith, the Word, and authority work together, releasing God's power upon the earth.

Then Jesus said to the centurion, 'Go your way; and as you have believed, so let it be done for you.' And his servant was healed that same hour. MATTHEW 8:13

Kingdom Keys

1. You have authority given to you by your Father in Heaven.

2. The Word of God holds all authority.

3. Your authoritative faith is enough.

9

Alive in Christ

Jesus said to her, "I am the resurrection and the life. Whoever believes in me, though he die, yet shall he live, and everyone who lives and believes in me shall never die. Do you believe this?"
JOHN 11:25-26

The Kingdom key I want to leave you with is the area of Resurrection Power. You have resurrection power inside of you! We all do! For those who believe, we hold the Kingdom of Heaven within us. Hopefully, you've established this for yourself as you've read this book. And if you need a little more convincing, let's look at the story of Lazarus.

When it seems we've arrived too late for something or someone, it can feel like an opportunity has passed us by. Or we might think we're just getting too old and too much time has gone by to see our promises and dreams from God come to pass in our lives. But I want to encourage you that even when Lazarus was dead upon Jesus' arrival, He was still perfectly on time.

As a Seer Prophet, when you've seen a thing, you know it's already been done. So, in my heart, mind, and belief system, when I see something, it's done; it's already happened. I have a close friend who's been wheelchair-bound for many years now, but I've seen him walking on more than one occasion when others and I have prayed for him. So, I know he will walk.

I also know more than ever that God's timing and way of bringing things to pass are entirely up to His Sovereign will and not ours. God's perfect timing is everything. We don't realise why some things take time or happen a certain way, but God knows. Our job is to trust Him through it and continue to believe.

Not everyone around you has the same faith you have, and you'll have to navigate through that. We saw this in the story of Jairus and his daughter, as well as in the story of Lazarus. When we talk about faith, we often speak of partnering with faith. I like to talk about partnering with the Holy Spirit in faith. In our salvation moment, we have faith to receive Jesus into our lives. The Word of God says we are to walk out our faith with fear and trembling. When we do this, in time, our faith will increase.

***

I've noticed a lot of Christians seem to struggle with navigating the process of death. In death, there's life, and life is eternal. Jesus raised Lazarus from the dead because his time was not over, and there was a lesson people needed to learn. Jewish tradition had room for dead people to come alive after three days, but on the fourth, that was unseen and unheard of. The miracle of his resurrection needed to happen and be a witness through the end of the ages. You see, it took longer than anyone expected for Jesus to arrive, and many felt he was too late to perform a miracle. But Jesus was right on time.

At the beginning of the book, I shared a dedication to my beautiful son, Shaun Connor Reynolds, who departed Earth on 18 October 2023. His death was sudden and very traumatic for not just our family but our fellow brothers and sisters in Christ, locally and globally. I took time to reflect after the funeral when everyone went home to their respective places. Sitting with the Lord, I reflected on Shaun's day of passing.

I expressed to God my uncertainty in sharing the details about the circumstances of his death because of the extensive nature of the events. I questioned which portion people needed to hear today. He revealed this is for those who know Christ as their Lord and Saviour. Those who know Christ need to listen to this part of my and my son's story, as God is still writing it. Even though Shaun is dead, he's not truly dead. He's alive in Christ. Death is an earthly realm. Life is eternal.

So, I want to pull the resurrection promise out of our story. The resurrection's power and promise hold great meaning for us believers in Christ, the Sons and Daughters of God. I now have God's unique perspective on resurrection and its significance. And I'd love to start by telling you who my son is because this story is about his life, not just his death.

***

At eighteen years old, Shaun walked to work along the railroad tracks one morning. No, he shouldn't have been there, but it's where he was because that's what he does. Tragically, a train collided with Shaun and killed him instantly with blunt force trauma (according to the coroner's initial findings). Shaun had Asperger's syndrome, and we recognised his differences from an early age, leading to his diagnosis during his primary years—now known as Autism Spectrum Disorder (ASD).

Shaun's perspective on life was incredible, and his insight was a gift from God. When he was four years old, I found him lying on the carpet, rolling around in the light's warmth, pouring in on him at an angle, coming through our big lounge room window. It was one of those moments as a mum that you see your children differently. It was as if God was shining a purposeful light, like a torch, directly on him. As I watched him roll and bask in the light of Christ, Holy Spirit spoke and told me to stop trying to fix him!

Everywhere we went, people wanted to lay hands on our kids and pray for them during our time as community pastors. They saw Shaun as different and often labelled him a problem child. Subsequently, he became our problem; in my mind, we had to fix him.

I had to seek God's word for healing, but the Lord told me to stop fixing and accept him as He created him to be. He said He prepared Shaun before time began and before he entered my womb. He was with him, and Shaun was everything He wanted him to be—an important message for any parent with a child slightly different from the rest. Be at peace because God creates our children. They're His children, and He merely lends them to us for a time.

***

Shaun grew up and became a joyful noise in our lives. My whole family is loud (that's my genes), but Shaun was extra loud and often obnoxious with it, with no social filters whatsoever. His lack of filters and discernment led to him walking on the train tracks that day. He felt invincible, and yet he was brilliant. He couldn't comprehend the danger because he'd calculated the train timetables and knew exactly when they ran. Unaware of the train's unscheduled training exercise, he didn't consider the risk of walking that way.

Shaun also had sensory issues, and walking on the muddy and slushy ground beside the tracks felt unsafe. Walking on the train tracks provided stability for his logical mind. That was his unique insight and perspective in action. When I explain it that way, you can understand his reasoning. It makes sense when you see it from his perspective. And it's that new perspective I want you to have as we unpack resurrection power.

For us, resurrection power is Jesus raising from the dead and Jesus raising Lazarus from the dead. But it's much more than we think. Jesus delivered Mary Magdalene from all her "stuff," and that's definitely resurrection power as well. We know that the name of Jesus heals broken hearts, and that's also resurrection power. Deliverance of the mind from insane to sane, alcoholism to sobriety, and from addiction to freedom is also resurrection power. The greatest miracle brings resurrection to our spirits, making us alive in Him (Galatians 2:20, 2 Corinthians 5:17).

Christians often solely focus on the cross and what Jesus accomplished there. But what was accomplished when Jesus rose from the grave—that's resurrection power. Jesus shared this with us. My perspective on resurrection power and what it means in the light of Shaun's death has shifted. We can move in greater faith as God's Word opens for us. Join me in exploring this, as I believe God is calling us to adopt a new perspective. Perhaps not a superior method, but certainly a more profound one.

Please pause and read John 11, in its fullness, before you continue.

***

In John 11, God introduces us to some interesting family dynamics. We have Mary and Martha, sisters, and Lazarus, their brother. Jesus is close to this family, and they love Him dearly. Take note that Jesus also loves your family dearly. When Jesus heard that his good friend Lazarus was sick, He spoke the end before he saw it and prophesied immediately. "This sickness is not unto death, but for the glory of God, that the Son of God may be glorified through it" (John 11:4).

In the family dynamic of God's Kingdom, where does your faith currently stand as a part of the royal family? Are you able to speak with the authority of Jesus? Can you prophesy over your brother or sister's cancer and call it cancelled in Jesus' name? Can you speak life over them, not death, as that will glorify God? Jesus did all the things and more!

***

Shaun listened to music at a thousand decibels per second (exaggeration) through a portable speaker held on his shoulder, blaring into his ears. He loved to do this. It was so loud you could hear him from many streets away. But because of this, his death was sudden and tragic. However, just like the story of Lazarus was for God's glory, Shaun's story is also for God's glory. No matter how painful it is to lose a child without reason or purpose, God will always get the glory. Regardless of the situation, we need to view it from that perspective.

A few months before writing this book, an incident occurred in which death took my son from Earth. But he's not dead; he's alive, and I'm okay with that. Yes, it's difficult; navigating through grief is extremely hard to do with so many emotions at play. Our extensive family has many young ones requiring guidance in navigating this grief. But we all agreed not to give the devil a foothold (Ephesians 4:27).

Some days, we cry; others, we get angry, laugh, and then cry again. We still talk about Shaun's weaknesses as much as his strengths as we remember him together as a family daily. Like ours, Lazarus' family had their own emotions, thoughts, and challenges to overcome. John 11 starts with the family of Lazarus. And Jesus is part of that family. Shaun's death begins with our family, but Jesus is also part of it.

***

We were all together the morning of the tragedy, getting ready for work, school, and a day of ministry. Everyone left, and I had just finished with an international ministry Zoom call. With a knock at my door, I opened it to find a very young and fidgety policeman doing his best to express to me that there had been an incident and that he needed to come into my home to speak with me. I knew straight away it was one of my children.

In times of trauma and tragedy, Jesus is in the midst of it all. Even when we can't see Him, He is there. Just as Lazarus' family gathered around him in the tragedy of what appeared to be severe illness and then death, when Jesus didn't arrive immediately, He was still there. God is always with us.

Within death, Jesus was raising our family back to life. I'm sure there are moments in your life that have resurrected your family. However estranged or difficult, I pray earnestly that any reconciliation or redemption is not just for a moment but remains a place of togetherness for a lifetime.

When the police arrived on my doorstep and shared the news, I asked first how they knew it was Shaun. An older policewoman gave me Shaun's passport and wallet, saying they were sure it was him. In my shock and disbelief, God stepped in. In my weakness, He became my strength. There's none so perfect that has walked this world but Jesus. And Jesus and I can assure you, the shock that set in made me something far less than perfect in that moment.

We're human and vulnerable, and we all have moments of weakness to overcome. Some are for the Lord to carry us, and others are there for us to rest in Him, to allow Him to simply carry us, as a good Father does. I sat at my dining table in complete shock, entering a supernatural realm for at least three days—resurrection timing. Reality ceased to exist during those days.

***

The police officers were still there with me on that first day, talking to me, and as I looked up, I saw an open portal. Standing before me was my father, who'd passed away several years prior, alongside Shaun. Together, they stood with their sides facing me, holding fishing poles. The significance was profound because they loved fishing but hadn't known that about each other. They hadn't had time to truly know each other on that level in earthly life, but there they were together, ready to fish.

As they turned towards me, my dad put his arm around Shaun's shoulder in an embrace, and they both smiled. That was another point of significance, as neither of them smiled much. Then my father spoke. "We're going fishing now." He gave me a nod, meaning everything was okay. Shaun's grin was massive, and I saw him so happy! Then they disappeared.

I knew the Bible to be confirmed at that moment because the Word tells us a great cloud of witnesses awaits us when we enter Heaven (Hebrews 12:1-3). The Bible is not just a good story; it's the truth; the Word of God is both revelatory and complete in truth. The Word wasn't just for 2,000+ years ago; it's for today; it's alive. The Word of God is living and active! How life is on earth is not how it will be in Heaven. Life is difficult, but Heaven has all the answers, and life is good. We do well to remember that there is no eternal suffering!

There's a promise for you that when you leave your physical body and go to your Heavenly Father, people will wait to welcome you in. Only those people and God knew what great comfort it would give me to see my father and son together, fishing, of all things! God knows what will bring you comfort amid a tragedy. And He wants to give us those special moments. Seeing them fishing was my comfort and peace. Within the moment of tragic news, it was the certainty of where my son now was.

> *And I am glad for your sakes that I was not there, that you may believe. Nevertheless, let us go to him.* JOHN 11:15

***

Some people thought Jesus was too late, and because of the time it took to get there, Lazarus passed away. However, Christ told his followers He was glad He hadn't arrived sooner. If He had, what would've happened? Things would have been so different. Jesus was right on time—right on time for a miracle, right on time for the resurrection power to be displayed and believed.

When Scripture says Lazarus was sick, perhaps our modern mindsets go straight to thinking about how it's just the flu. How bad can it be? But we know that even what appears to be the flu can be life-threatening and very serious. Lazarus was so sick that those around him thought he might die, and then he did! Jesus, however, had already spoken a word about the situation. And there it is again, that spoken authority. This was not unto death (John 11:4).

Do you think the disciples were questioning Jesus' reliability at this stage and losing trust in His word? He said it wasn't unto death, but hello, Lazarus looks dead to us! You said one thing, but we cannot deny what is right in front of us. Do you think they trusted Him? Is He the real deal, or what? They certainly couldn't deny what they saw!

If Jesus had been any earlier, we know a healing would've occurred. But this event was for specific people to witness the glory of God. Those who needed to see would believe! But hold that thought for a moment. After I processed the fact that Shaun was dead, my husband arrived home, and we told our other children of their brothers' passing. The Spirit of God rose in me and took over during that time.

> *It is no longer I that lives, but Christ who lives in me.*
> GALATIANS 2:20

Ephesians 3:15-17 speaks of how every name in heaven and earth derives its name from God. We are called family because we all belong to God. You know your family members. You know when they are hurting. When one goes into pain in the Body of Christ, we all feel it.

The morning of Shaun's death, our two armour bearers, intercessors from my local church, rushed to our side. They sprang into action without hesitation. I said I needed to touch my son. I just needed to touch him. That's not normal for me to say, but the Spirit of God took over. I wasn't thinking that I needed to touch him to raise him from the dead. I was sure of where he was. My eyes saw the Glory of the Lord. Shaun had landed in heaven and arrived home. I knew that. I had comfort and peace, but a driving force within me was strong. My spirit man cried out, telling me I needed to touch him. Then there was the reality of the police trying to tell me nicely that I probably didn't really want to go and touch him.

Blunt force trauma by train. You can only imagine what that might mean. The police were just trying their best to protect me from the horror they knew lay under the covers where his broken body lay. Their wisdom and experience told them this would not be a good thing for me to witness, trying to spare me from the difficult moment of seeing Shaun's body. But his spirit had left, and I felt a powerful urge to firmly instruct them not to remove the body until we had prayed on the land where the train struck him and until I had touched my son!

As I exercised that authority, there was an expanse of space in the spiritual and natural realms. Heaven and earth rearranged themselves to make it possible for me to see and touch Shaun's body. On a natural level, I ponder that perhaps somewhere deep in my subconscious, I longed for his physical touch because we had not had our usual hug that morning. Maybe I needed that last parting connection before saying goodbye in person.

***

I'm bold at the best of times, but when the Spirit of the Lord takes over, commanding and demanding, the anointing of boldness is clearly present. God tells us when certain things must occur. We don't know why, but we obey obediently, even in the most difficult circumstances.

With our pastors now also at our side, we prayed at the site of the accident while the police and the rail company were still collecting and removing Shaun's body from the train tracks. As we gathered together, I fell to my knees, praying in tongues, hitting the ground, with the train company and first responders bearing witness. I prayed according to the Lord, and some of what I prayed I couldn't even tell you. The sounds and words flowed out of me like living waters as the Spirit of the Lord continued overcoming me.

My husband gripped my hand as I kneeled and pressed into the land. Then he hit the ground, too, and at that moment, our pastors and armour bearers saw in the spirit what they described as an explosion. As both our knees hit the land simultaneously, it was as if the heavens opened. I saw an angel appear, swiping an extremely large sword across the land.

Later, an apostle in our nation said it was as if our son had served as an atonement for the area, and the land was now open to receive the Gospel. Since our son's death, our entire community has been deeply affected. It's like a veil has lifted, and sharing Christ with people has become easier. Not that it was difficult before, but there's a newfound flow.

We received testimony from one of the armour bearers who says he saw a gold ring appear in the heavens with a cape pulled through it. A cap appeared, and he heard the word graduate. He whispered to me softly that my son had graduated. This was another confirmation and a beautiful blessing to receive the word that Shaun still lives.

The veil between life and death is so wonderful. Christians often talk about places as heavenly realms, but I now know *we* are the heavenly realms. We carry the Kingdom of God within us. God has told me that wherever I go and my feet step, the land is given to me, and that territory is mine. That I possess it, and God's glory lives within it. Let us remember that we carry the Kingdom of God.

> *And I heard a loud voice from the throne saying, "Look! God's dwelling place is now among the people, and he will dwell with them. They will be his people, and God himself will be with them and be their God.* REVELATION 21:3 *NIV*

Afterword
Call to Arise

I had a dream. In my dream, I saw a young girl wearing a dull-looking white dress that seemed worn out and needed a good wash. She was lying down and appeared to be sleeping. Jesus entered her room, approached her, bent down, and brushed her hair aside from her forehead. Then he stood up and looked at her for a moment.

With compassion and love, Jesus bent down and gently kissed her head in the same spot. She remained asleep, and He left quietly. I heard Holy Spirit clear as day. *Talitha Cumi*. Then I woke up.

This was such an intimate moment that I initially felt the dream was just for me and Jesus. I thought perhaps I was the little girl Jesus was comforting. That would make sense because I had been deeply mourning my son Shaun. But the longer the dream simmered, and as I spoke the vision out, it became a greater revelation for the wider Church.

Seeing through a wider lens, I see the little girl as representative of the Church's immature state right now. She was alone, isolated, and seemingly without parents. I sensed she was not well. Over time, her clothing had become sullied and needed cleaning. I feel how deeply Jesus cared for the child in her state of illness. In Mark 5:41, Jesus spoke the exact words that I heard. Talitha Cumi is translated as "Little girl, I say to you, arise."

The child in Mark 5 belonged to the ruler of the synagogue. Think for a moment about how the little girl belonged to the religious leader of the day. There was a great commotion and weeping over her death. And then Jesus made everyone leave the building except for the girl's parents—another example of

Jesus acknowledging parental authority. Jesus spoke to the girl, and she rose from the dead. Once again, there's the power of God's spoken word at work!

I believe the Lord is speaking to us through this dream: There's a generation of immature believers without mature spiritual mothers and fathers at this hour. They are becoming unwell, and some of what they have been operating in has become sullied, defiling the garments of the Church. The pure white garments that have become discoloured over time represent our giftings.

Jesus has come because He cares so deeply. He wants the mature ones, the mothers and fathers of the faith, to wake up and stand on His word. He wants them to stand in their authority, calling the immature church to arise and walk with them so they can be made well. If the mothers and fathers of faith intercede in this way, they will become the Risen Ones they are supposed to be in their generation.

Declare:

Talitha Cumi! ARISE!

Today is the day of resurrection power. It begins with us.

Sharon Reynolds

About the Author

Sharon Reynolds is the Regional Director for Women on the Frontlines New Zealand, impacting nations with her innovative programs, ideas, expertise, and leadership. She is a creative entrepreneur, an exhibited artist, an accomplished writer, and a wife, mother, and grandmother. Sharon is of Ngati Kahangunu and Te Arawa descent (indigenous to New Zealand). Sharon's work has taken her into the high schools and prisons of Aotearoa and Africa and into Cambodia, where she has worked with children rescued from trafficking. Her unique programs and workshops use mixed modalities that offer hope. Sharon works to bring justice to those living with injustice and to see people and communities transformed by love and the redeeming power of Christ.

Other Books by Sharon Reynolds
Available at online retailers worldwide

10

Glory Realms

Praise be to the God and Father of our Lord Jesus Christ! In his great mercy he has given us new birth into a living hope through the resurrection of Jesus Christ from the dead, and into an inheritance that can never perish, spoil or fade. This inheritance is kept in heaven for you, who through faith are shielded by God's power until the coming of the salvation that is ready to be revealed in the last time. 1 PETER 1:3-5

Shaun dedicated his life to Jesus as a little boy, and at eight years old, he asked to be water baptised. The pastor at the time wouldn't do it, saying he was too young. As a teenager, he was involved in many things, having to overcome a lot of hard stuff. He struggled. He always struggled a little in life. But as a teen, he *really* struggled. He just wanted to fit in. He wanted to belong. Like most teens, he wanted to be accepted. In Christ, he had that acceptance, but young people must figure out for themselves where they fit in and belong, and that's where he was on his journey.

He used to share with me how he no longer believed in God. He'd explain the most amazing things to me, incredibly complex revelations of science and fact. He had incredible insight, wisdom, and knowledge beyond his years. He nearly knocked a pastor off his pulpit once, in the middle of a youth meeting, when he encircled him and required an answer to "Well, tell me. Where did all the dinosaurs go then? What happened to them? Can you explain this to me, along with the mysteries of God? I want answers!"

When someone passes away, you wonder where they are. But my daughter brought something to my mind: He gave his heart to the Lord, and that never changes. The visions we saw and the ones others shared comforted us. As parents, there's a strong sense that God gave us these visions to show us exactly where Shaun is and assure us he is with Jesus. This assurance comforts us and gives us peace.

***

Now comes the resurrection part! Because of my insistence on touching Shaun's body, they pulled up the vehicle they had him in, and the undertaker presented his body to me, encased in a velvet vessel. She put down the back of the car and invited me to sit by him. She showed me the areas I could touch and explained which way was up. I could take my time and sit with my son. She told me where everything was from head to toe and asked how far I wanted to go with touching the body. She described the position of his head at the top, his arms beside him, and his feet at the end. He was still zipped up and completely encased.

The undertaker was really very lovely. I inquired why there was a box shape where his head was. She gently clarified that the box was holding his head in place due to the trauma it had experienced. It needed to be that way to keep what was remaining intact.

She never once offered to unzip the velvet vessel. But I kept telling her I needed to touch my son. She told me she knew what I was communicating and understood the reasoning. She showed me where to put my hand. Later, I found out she was a Christian.

She showed me the exact place that would be good for me to reach, and she tried to spare me unnecessary pain. Then she told me she would stand off to the side, giving me space and time, waiting until I was ready for her to take my boy to the hospital. My pastor's wife stood with me, and I touched the vessel he was in. As I did, his body felt warm. That didn't seem quite right. I leaned over to my pastor's wife and asked her if the body was supposed to be warm. She wasn't sure herself but agreed it would surely be cold by now; however, it wasn't. It was warm!

We stood there looking at each other, oddly amazed and unsure of what to do. I reached out again and touched Shaun, gently stroking the outer casing of the vessel, telling my son I loved him—and then the body moved suddenly! The power of God flooded through me, and under my hand, Shaun's body moved like a wave of wobbly jello (jelly). I was a bit startled, looking at my support person in shock. I returned my hand to the same position, and it happened again. A power surge of softness but strength went directly under my hand. Twice? That's no accident! I looked straight at the face of the woman standing next to me and squealed.

I asked if she saw what had happened, and she confirmed with wonder in her eyes that she had seen my hand move. She asked what we should do after that. We were both totally freaking out, neither of us knowing what to do, both of us in shock and completely baffled by what had just occurred, unsure of the reality of it.

***

Now, I can confidently tell you that I am a woman full of faith. I can believe for anything in Christ. I've overcome a cancer prognosis before it took full flight in my body. I've overcome death from a serious encounter with dengue fever, along with all kinds of tragedy and situations of suffering in my and my family's lives. I can testify to the power of God—no problem at all! I can pray, stand, and believe with you for anything with a Lion's roar in my spirit because I know my God. I know what He can do. But at that moment I didn't know what to do!

Christians say all the time when people get hurt or are on their deathbeds that we're going to be by their side. We say we're going into prayer, going to go to the morgues, and doing this and that, but will you actually do it? Will you really? Will you be the one who goes? Will you know what to do?

These times of trials are tests of who we say we are, what we truly believe in, and how far we will go. I had dreams about sneaking into the morgue and raising the dead. My kids know me so well they begged me not to do it! I could if I wanted to. I'm sure God would move everybody out of the way. If it were His will, He would have every opposition and barrier laid low, and a way would open for me to go.

What was the will of God in this situation? You might think that the will of God is for us to live and not to die, and yet Shaun was dead but also alive. That's the part you have to wrap your head around. He's alive; he's *not* dead. When we talk about Jesus, the risen Jesus, and the resurrection, we talk about how He's alive; He is *not* dead.

So, just because someone's body is no longer partaking in the earth, it does not mean that they're not still living. It also doesn't mean we have free license just to lay hands on everybody in the morgue and bring them back. God has a purpose in death as much as He does in life. Remember, Jesus died so all may live.

Sometimes, we get full of religion and religious ways, and our Christianese (yes, that's an actual language, not a typo) takes over. We must push that aside and believe in God's miraculous resurrection power. But we also need to listen to the Lord, move when He says to move and do what He says to do. In Lazarus's case, Jesus told the disciples that the situation was for the Glory of God. "I am right on time." Believe.

***

The undertaker returned to where we stood, and I asked her a simple question. "When somebody dies like this, does their body get cold, or does it take time for the fluid and all that to settle down?" I had technical questions that my logical brain needed to resolve to make sense of what just happened. She confirmed the body was stone cold. Shaun had been deceased for several hours now, and his body was freezing. I explained that I touched him, and he was not cold but that he was, in fact, warm to the touch. Knowing after the event that she was a believer in Christ, her response makes more sense. "Oh yes, they stay warm to the touch of those who believe."

Who would know that God was setting us up in the best of ways? I carried on asking, "When you touch a dead person's body, could it be like waves, kind of like getting on a waterbed? When you touch them, is the fluid supposed to move? Is that how it all works? Is this how it goes, and is it normal?" I've since asked many other people to clarify this as well. I was blown away by what I saw and needed proof. The undertaker informed me that fluids do not move under your hands like a waterbed moving. I knew then that this experience was exactly what I thought it to be.

She packed up the vehicle, headed off, and I headed home. I had only one question for the Lord that day. I wanted to know why that happened. I wasn't questioning why Shaun died so young or why he got hit by a train. These are not the usual questions you might expect. No, I had just one question for God. *Did I miss it, Lord?*

Had I missed the moment of resurrection? Why did God allow that? Did I get it wrong? Could I have raised my son from the dead, and I missed it in shock? Or was this my unbelief that I needed to deal with? What's going on, and what just happened?

Holy Spirit responded to my inquiry with reverence and complete holiness. He told me He allowed it so I would know it was possible. In John 11:15, when the Lord told the disciples that Jesus raised Lazarus from the dead so they would believe, perhaps He was actually implying that it had to happen that way for them to believe. I now know that God wants us to step into a new realm of His glory, and as we do, we'll step into new opportunities that will awaken our spirit. We'll no longer question if we're manufacturing the things of God, but we'll gladly be able to follow His lead, knowing the power we carry and what it's for.

***

This Dumanis power is for raising dead hearts and minds, dead lives physically, spiritually, and financially: these things and more. We can become so fixated on the body with resurrection power, but when the raising of Lazarus from the dead happened, it saved an entire community. A whole nation was impacted by Lazarus' resurrection story, which still impacts nations today.

Like Lazarus' family, our whole family has now experienced resurrection power. After Shaun's funeral, many young people approached us to tell stories of how Shaun impacted their lives. They wanted us to know that because of him, they were following Jesus. We were genuinely astounded but very blessed to know that Jesus in Shaun had been at work in miraculous ways in the lives of many.

We televised Shaun's funeral online as many people wanted to be there but couldn't for a variety of reasons, including distance. People we'd never met or even knew contacted us after the service to say how much his story touched them. Some gave their lives to Jesus during the funeral, and many returned to God, whom they had abandoned years before. Hundreds of people sent us messages, expressing how encouraged they were by our collective family story amid our valley of grief.

***

My husband and I shared with our family what occurred at the site of Shaun's death. We told them about the resurrection power I experienced. Our youngest daughter confirmed she was so moved and shaken that she was turning her life around to get things right with God. Her revelation blessed our hearts. She believes in God, worships Him, and prays to Him. She loves the Lord with all her heart. But she expressed that her worshipping may look different from ours, and we must be okay with that. It is.

This next generation has a unique expression of belief. What I've learned through my son's death is that we cannot hinder the flow of God. He is Sovereign and moving in them, regardless of what we think it should look like! That's resurrection power. That's the power of God. There was never anything I could say to turn my daughter's life around, but God does the impossible with our children. He resurrects the deadest of hearts, and in death, there is life. Amen.

The word resurrection means to live again. I was dead, but now I live. God raises the dead areas inside your heart to a risen life in Him. When we stop judging and criticising the generation after us and instead recognise them as dedicated followers and lovers of Jesus, we will witness our inheritance coming alive through them.

Love conquers everything. God's love has carried us through this tragic time in our lives. Christ's love caused Lazarus, his family, and an entire community to live again. God's love sent Elisha and Elijah to speak into the desperate women's lives. And the love and compassion of Christ saw the centurion's servant healed, and the women afflicted for years with a crippling blood issue able to walk in complete freedom.

God's love turns the worst of situations back around. His love covers us in the most challenging moments of life. Even when we walk through tragedy and trauma, the valley of the shadow of death, He is there.

***

We don't stop loving someone just because they're not in the room with us. So it is with Christ. I love Jesus. He turned me around, saved me, and brought me back to life. His love lives in each of us. Right now, Jesus loves you. He loved Martha, Mary, and Lazarus. And now He loves you, as He always has.

Love sees. Love knows. Love asks. Love responds.

Mary and Martha called for Jesus out of love. "If light is not in them, people stumble in life." If you don't have Jesus, you will stumble. That's just the truth. Life is hard. Jesus woke Lazarus, physically and spiritually—I believe that's what we're to do as believers—this is our mandate and calling as we walk into the next era.

Jesus is calling us to wake the dead, to use the resurrection's Dunamis power, imparted to us as children of God, and to believe in Him with such strength and virtue that we can go anywhere in this world and see people's lives transformed through a loving moment with Jesus. I'm here today, sharing my experiences and writing these stories so that verse 15 will come to life for you: "So that you may know and believe it's possible."

My belief is greater than ever before because of my son's life, death, and all God has allowed and shown me. I've entered a new realm of authority and belief to glorify God. It's now time for you to believe in resurrection power. Do you believe?

***

A few months after Shaun's death, a neighbour came running to my door, excitedly recounting a dream she'd just woken from. She saw Jesus riding on a white horse. He went past her, looked at her, and smiled. Sadly, her son passed away a few years ago, and in her dream, he came riding in hot on the heels of

Jesus. Riding on another horse was her grandson, who'd also passed on. Finally, Shaun followed them all. Wearing chain mail armour, he turned, looked, and grinned at her.

She recalled how his face shone and noticed he wasn't wearing his glasses. When she shared this, I felt Holy Spirit drop in on me, saying Shaun doesn't need the glasses now because he has been made perfect. In Heaven, there's no pain or suffering. In Christ, we attain perfection. I burst into tears on my doorstep that day and praised God for His love. My son is not dead but surely alive!

Kingdom Keys

1. You hold resurrection power.

2. Your story will impact nations.

3. Your legacy is resurrection, and your inheritance is power.

4. Love is the key.

5. You are risen, and your story is still being written. It's not over!

Jesus told Lazarus' sister that He is both resurrection and life. He who believes in Me, though he may die, he shall live. And whoever lives and believes in Me shall never die (John 11: 25-26). Do you believe this? Do we believe we shall never die as we believe in Christ?

In conclusion, I want to leave you with the thought that God has placed resurrection power inside you. Then I want to ask you a question. What will you do with it?

As I finished the last sentences of this chapter, I encountered a young man whose friend had just committed suicide. He was struggling and finding it hard to stay focused on living. Merely listening to him turned out to be so much more. I was able to speak life into him. Several days later, he came to me and expressed his sincerest gratitude for talking to him with truth and wisdom. He now understands why he had to attend the event where we met. God led him to me that day. And the word God gave me for him freed his heart and mind from the internal prison he was in. He experienced a resurrection!

> *For God so loved the world that He gave His only begotten Son, that whoever believes in Him should not perish but have everlasting life. For God did not send His Son into the world to condemn the world, but that the world through Him might be saved.* JOHN 3:16-17

I celebrate with people worldwide with joy, embracing God's resurrection power and bringing transformation from darkness to life. You are the Risen One! You have the same power as God! As His family, we're supposed to speak life because we hold the keys to life! I leave you with this truth from Revelation 1:18: "I am He who lives, and was dead, and behold, I am alive forevermore. Amen. And I have the keys of Hades and of Death."

Remember, God is still writing your story, my story, and Shaun's story. It's not over yet. Stay strong as your story is still unfolding.

www.ingramcontent.com/pod-product-compliance
Lightning Source LLC
Chambersburg PA
CBHW050437010526
44118CB00013B/1574